Please return or renew this item by the last date shown.

Libraries Line and Renewals: **020 7361 3010**

Web Renewals: www.rbkc.gov.uk/renewyourbooks

KENSINGTON AND CHELSEA LIBRARY SERVICE

Honor Head

First published in Great Britain in 2019
by The Watts Publishing Group
10 9 8 7 6 5 4 3 2 1

Editor: Nicola Edwards
Cover design: Lisa Peacock and Thy Bui
Inside design: Matthew Lilly
Cover and inside illustrations
by Roberta Terracchio
Consultant: Clare Arnold, psychotherapist with 25 years'
experience working with CAMHS, the NHS's Child and
Adolescent Mental Health Services)

ISBN 978 1 4451 6471 7 (HB); 978 1 4451 6472 4 (PB)
Printed in China

Franklin Watts
An imprint of
Hachette Children's Group
Part of the Watts Publishing Group
Carmelite House
50 Victoria Embankment
London EC4Y 0DZ
An Hachette UK Company
www.hachette.co.uk
www.franklinwatts.co.uk

WHAT IS A TRUSTED ADULT?

Throughout the book we suggest you speak to a trusted adult. This is a person who makes you feel safe and that you can trust. It could be a parent or carer or another family member, such as an aunt or uncle or grandparent. It could be a teacher or someone you know well, such as a family friend or a friend's parent or carer. Or it could be someone at the end of a helpline (see pages 46-47).

CONTENTS

DREAM TEAM!

Your brain and body work as a team. What you do with your body affects your mood, while your thoughts and feelings affect how you feel physically.

BLINK, BREATHE, CHEW!

Can you think of things your body does without you having to think about it. For example:

speaking

blinking

chewing and swallowing food

shivering

sweating

It does all these things with the help of your brain. Your brain is working 24 hours a day, every day you're alive – even while you're asleep. But your brain doesn't run the show alone; it is helped by your nervous system. The nervous system is a complicated bundle of nerves inside your spine. These nerves connect to every part of your body, from your eyes to your toes. Your body and brain use the nervous system to send messages back and forth to each other all the time.

RED ALERT

Your nervous system is always on red alert. If something dangerous is about to happen, such as if a ball is speeding towards you or you're about to touch a hot pan, your brain and nervous system react immediately and make you dodge the ball or pull your hand back from the hot pan.

NEURON POWER

We're born with a brain and nervous system so why don't we automatically know how to read or walk or ride a bike?

When you're born your brain is equipped with millions and millions of neurons made up of cells. Each neuron has tiny branches coming from it that can connect to other neurons … a bit like lots of people reaching out and holding hands to form a line. The neurons start to connect when you start to learn things, when you learn to walk, talk, read, play football, dance. Once you start to learn the neurons make connections so that the activity becomes easier and easier until you do it automatically.

TRY THIS!

Look out for these boxes throughout this book. They will give you hints and tips on quick ways to improve your emotional and physical health that you can try every day or whenever you need to.

HELLO, BRAIN!

So now we know how important the brain is, let's have a quick look at how it works.

THE CEREBRUM

The biggest part of the brain is called the cerebrum and it's the part that controls your voluntary muscles. So when you play football, dance or just get out of a chair, this part of your brain is working to get the muscles you need to move. The cerebrum also helps you to think. It helps you do your homework and figure out how to win a video game. That's not all. It also controls your memory and reasoning, such as deciding whether something is a good or a bad thing to do.

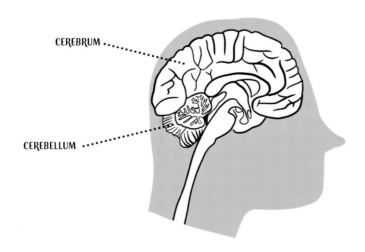

CEREBRUM

CEREBELLUM

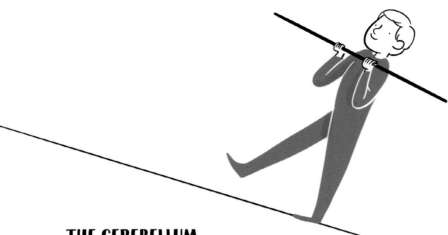

THE CEREBELLUM

Whether you're skateboarding,
surfing or just walking in a straight line, you
need your cerebellum to keep your balance and
coordination. This is the bit of the brain that controls
how your muscles work together.

THE BRAIN STEM

Your brain stem is connected to your spine and keeps
you alive. It is in charge of your involuntary muscles, all
those muscles inside you that you never think about
such as your heart and muscles around your lungs that
keep you breathing.

THE PITUITARY GLAND

This part of the brain is especially important to preteens. The pituitary gland is only the size of a pea but it has a massive effect on your body when you reach puberty. During puberty the pituitary gland releases hormones into your body that start your physical body changes as you grow and develop into an adult (see page 10).

EMOTIONS CENTRE

It's not just your actions that your brain controls. It also controls the way you feel, your moods and emotions. Whenever you feel sad, happy, disappointed, angry, scared or any other emotion, these feelings are coming from a part of your brain called the amygdala (say: uh-mig-dah-lah).

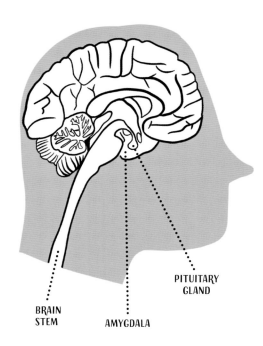

PITUITARY GLAND

BRAIN STEM

AMYGDALA

BRAIN CARE

So now you know how important your brain is, you can see how it's important to look after it as much as it is to look after your body. As we'll see in this book, what you do to your body affects your brain, and how you use your brain affects your body. Your physical health and mental health are closely linked.

HORMONE HAVOC!

Puberty creates hormone changes in the brain. These not only affect your body but also the way you think and feel.

PHYSICAL CHANGES

During puberty your body changes from a child's body into an adult's. You might have growth spurts, where parts of your body like your arms and legs suddenly grow much faster. Boys start to develop muscles, their chest and shoulders become broader and they start to get more body hair especially on their chest.

Girls start to develop rounder hips, their breasts start to grow and some girls may grow more body hair. Both boys and girls might start to sweat and smell more. All these physical changes are perfectly normal.

MENTAL CHANGES

All the hormones that flood your body during puberty also affect your brain and your moods and emotions. This can lead to huge mood swings – one minute you can feel on top of the world, the next you might hate everybody and think everybody hates you!

The hormones will affect each person differently. You might feel suddenly irritable and grumpy, the smallest thing might make you feel like shouting and slamming doors, you might think no one understands you, that everyone's against you and the world has suddenly become a strange and frustrating place.

EMOTION COMMOTION

Some young people becoming teenagers might also feel sad and anxious about what is happening to them or in the world around them. These mixed emotions can make you feel even more worried and maybe a bit frightened about what is happening to you. What you are feeling is all perfectly natural. However, if you do feel overwhelmed by sadness, anger, anxiety or by your feelings and if your moods are affecting your schoolwork and ability to enjoy life, you may need to speak to a trusted adult and see a doctor to make sure everything is okay. Don't be ashamed or embarrassed to ask for help; puberty is a challenging time and everyone reacts to it in their own way.

TRY THIS!

If you feel as if your head is about to explode or is filled with bad thoughts, try to calm your body and mind by doing a simple breathing exercise. Find a quiet place. Breathe in through your nose for a count of four. Hold it for a couple of seconds, breathe out through your mouth for a count of five. Repeat until you feel calmer.

EAT WELL

What you eat not only keeps your body and brain healthy, it can affect your moods and how you cope with everything.

GETTING IT RIGHT

Eating the right amount of food and the right type of food keeps your body in good condition and your brain healthy. It also helps you to cope with mood swings and negative emotions when they do happen. A healthy diet is one that includes a lot of fruit and vegetables, some protein such as meat, fish, lentils and beans or vegetarian protein such as tofu, and carbohydrates such as brown pasta and rice. Try and keep sweet things such as ice cream and cakes for special treats.

HOW DOES WHAT I EAT AFFECT MY BRAIN?

We've seen how your brain has a lot of work to do and to do it properly it needs the right fuel. Nutrients, such as vitamins and minerals, from food give you energy to keep yourself going and to grow and develop properly. These nutrients also keep all the nerves and neurons in top condition so you can concentrate on schoolwork and learning. A healthy diet helps to keep the parts of your brain that control your emotions and moods in good working order, too.

A diet overloaded with fast food or ready-made meals, that contain lots of sugar and chemical additives, can make you feel sluggish, anxious and grumpy. A healthy diet makes you feel alert and happy and helps you to cope with everyday stresses much better.

WELL WATERED

Your body needs water to stay healthy and so does your brain. Water also keeps your brain sharp and stops you feeling tired, fuzzy and muddled. If we get dehydrated it makes us feel irritable and grumpy. Keeping well hydrated improves concentration, helps us to stabilise our moods and feelings, eliminates toxins from the blood, keeps brain cells healthy, helps us sleep better and improves blood flow and oxygen to the brain. Wow! How much water you need to drink depends on your age, weight and how active you are. Drink a glass of water with meals and when you feel thirsty. If you're being active or it's warm, make sure you have water with you. As well as drinking water, you get water from fruit and vegetables so have plenty of these in your diet. Sugary drinks don't count!

TRY THIS!

If you have trouble remembering to drink water, get in the routine of having a glass or mug of water when you get up in the morning and one before you go to bed.

ISSUES WITH EATING

There are many reasons why some people develop eating disorders.

WHAT ARE EATING DISORDERS?

Two eating disorders you may have heard of are anorexia nervosa, when someone believes they are overweight so stops eating or eats very little, and bulimia nervosa. Bulimia is when a person stuffs themselves with food and then purges themselves – makes themselves sick or takes laxatives to go to the loo a lot. Food binging or compulsive eating is similar, but the person may not purge themselves. All eating disorders seriously damage a person's health and in some cases can even be fatal.

WHY DO THEY HAPPEN?

Eating disorders can happen when a person has experienced an emotional trauma, such as a family breaking up, being put into foster care or someone dying. Developing an eating disorder is a way for that person to feel they are in control of their lives by controlling the food they eat, when the world around them has become out of control and a frightening place.

Every day we are
bombarded with images
of slim, glamorous
people who seem
to have the perfect
lifestyle. This can make
some people think that
if they were slimmer
they would be happier,
have more friends
and a better life. They
start to obsess about
their weight and what
they eat, and this
develops into an eating
disorder. Some children
have parents who are
weight-obsessed and
this passes on food
anxieties to the children.

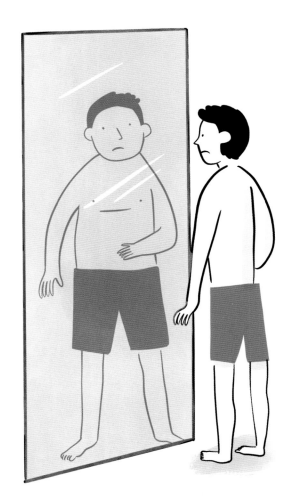

GETTING HELP

Whatever the reason for an eating disorder, if you think
you might have one it is essential to get professional
help. There is no need to feel scared or ashamed to talk
to someone.

Speak to a trusted adult or phone a helpline (see pages 46-47) and make sure you get some medical advice. If you think a friend has an eating disorder and they won't do anything, speak to a trusted adult on behalf of the friend or suggest that the friend speaks to an adult they trust. The sooner your friend gets help the sooner they'll get better.

> "
> *When my parents started to argue I would grab handfuls of food and sit in my room and eat and eat until I felt sick while I heard them shouting at each other. Eating and then being sick became a way to cope with unhappy things, and I found I was binge eating if I got poor test results, had a silly argument with my friends or any small thing really. Eventually my parents split up and I rang a helpline about my eating. I talked to Mum and we went to see the doctor. I'm not binge eating so much now and I feel much better mentally and physically.*
>
> Stuart, 15
> "

SELF-ESTEEM

**What we think of ourselves
is a good indication of our
mental health.**

ALL MY FAULT!

Self-esteem is what we think of ourselves. Self-esteem is about liking and trusting ourselves, and being proud of who we are. Most of us, for all sorts of reasons, can be very hard on ourselves. We think we're not good looking enough. We're no good at art or useless at sport. Our schoolwork is not good enough and we are always embarrassing ourselves. If we don't get picked for a school team, lose a game or a friend dumps us, it's our fault. But let's face it, not everything can be one person's fault!

POSITIVE BOUNCE BACK

People with good self-esteem will be positive thinkers, ready to give anything a try. People with low self-esteem think they will fail before they've even started and imagine no one will like them or want to be their friend so why try. It's not easy, but you can change how you feel by how you think. If you ever think "this is too hard", or "I can't do this", stamp out the negative thoughts and think, "I can do this", "I'll give it a try". Even if you don't get it quite right, you'll feel better about yourself because you tried. Remember we talked about neuron power in your brain (pages 5-6)? Well, the more you say "I can" and "I'll try", the easier it will become and before you know it you'll be trying things without even having to think about it.

LOVE YOURSELF

You are special and unique. There really is no one else like you. Think about what makes you special – it might be your great sense of humour, kindness, willingness to help, or being a good listener.

If there is something about how you look that's troubling you, think about whether you can change it in some way. If you can't, you can decide to accept it and focus on what you like about the way you look, such as your lovely nails, great hair or nice eyes. Spend time with friends and family who love you and make you feel special and safe.

TRY THIS!

It may seem a bit strange at first, but give yourself three compliments a day that have nothing to do with how you look. It could be that you made a great sandwich for lunch, finished a test at school, made your friend laugh or offered to help in the kitchen. Soon your brain will become tuned in to more positive thoughts.

BODY IMAGE

A positive body image is linked to your self-esteem and how you feel about yourself.

MEDIA GLOSS

On television, in magazines and online we see celebrities and models, both male and female, who look perfect. But life just isn't like that. These images and online videos have been prepared, filtered, glossed and tweaked to look the way they do. This doesn't stop many of us comparing ourselves to the images we see all around us and

thinking we should be prettier, have bigger muscles, longer legs and flatter stomachs. We begin to hate the way we look and this becomes a negative body image. A negative body image is not just about how you look, it can affect your whole life.

You can begin to think that if only you were thinner, or taller or had smoother skin you'd be happier, have more friends and a lot more fun.

SOCIAL MEDIA

Nasty comments about how you look on social media can also affect your body image. If the comments are deliberate this is a form of bullying. If this happens to you tell a trusted adult or phone a helpline (see pages 46-47). There is no need to be ashamed; it is the bully who needs to be ashamed. Talking will help you to realise that what is being said is untrue and stop you feeling isolated. Block anyone who is being abusive – this takes away their power and helps you regain control.

HOW DO YOU KNOW IF YOU'VE GOT A BODY IMAGE PROBLEM?

Do you:

* Think about how you look all the time?

* Always comment on people's weight or their shape?

* Refuse food or go hungry because you think you need to lose weight?

If you said yes to any of these, it could be that you need to have think about how you see yourself. For a start, learn to be proud of your body – after all, it can do amazing things. Be proud that you are strong and healthy. If you do think you might be overweight, speak to a trusted adult and see a doctor to check out that everything is okay. If you want to be fitter, set yourself some goals and plan a routine. Setting yourself goals and achieving them will make you feel better mentally, and you'll be physically fitter too.

YOU ARE NOT PERFECT

No one is perfect. You need to accept that you may not be perfect but that you have lots of very special qualities that have nothing to do with the way you look. When you start to worry about how you look, think about something you do well or really enjoy, such as being with your best friend, looking after your pet, trampolining or football.

"

I was worried about being unfit as I don't like the sport we have to do at school. I enjoy watching kung-fu movies and my mum suggested that I try out some different martial arts to see if I'd like doing them as much as watching them. Now I go to judo every week. It's made me much fitter and I feel a lot healthier too. I love it!

Alex, 13

"

SWEET DREAMS!

Getting enough sleep
and good quality sleep is
important for us mentally
and physically.

WHY IS SLEEP SO IMPORTANT?

Young people need long periods of sleep
each night to help their body and brain
to grow and develop. While your body is
resting, your brain can focus on filing away
what has happened during the day. During
sleep the cells and neurons in your brain
are strengthened and renewed, helping
to improve concentration and memory.
Scientists have proved that sleep helps us to
learn better and remember more. Experts
believe a young person aged between 9 and
11 needs about 9.5 hours of sleep a night.

TIRED AND MOODY

Not getting enough sleep can also affect your moods. If you haven't slept well you can feel tired, grumpy and irritable the next day. It is harder to feel positive and upbeat when you are tired, and this could lead to negative thinking and dark moods. You are also more likely to make mistakes if you are tired, which can make you angry or affect your self-esteem.

A good night's sleep means you wake up feeling refreshed, energized, positive and looking forward to a new day.

SLEEP ZONE

Try these tips to make your room
a better place for a good night's sleep.

✱ Turn off your computer and phone an hour before
bed as the blue light from digital screens can
overstimulate areas of the brain making it more
difficult to sleep. Instead choose a book by your
favourite author and have a read before you sleep.

✱ Make sure you are comfortable – not too hot
or too cold.

✱ Try to go to bed at the same time every night so
that your brain and body get into a routine.

✱ Be active and try not to nap during the day.
But don't do anything too energetic just
before bedtime!

TRY THIS!

*If you can't sleep because you're worrying
about something, see if these tips help:*

● *Take your worry and lock it in a worry box (in your
head). Say you'll take it out and look at it again in
the morning.*

● *Write your worry down on paper and then tear it into
little pieces or crumple it into a ball and throw it away.*

● *Decide you will talk to someone about your worries
in the morning. This will make you feel better as you
now have a plan of action to deal with the problem.
This puts you back in control. Sweet dreams!*

ALWAYS TIRED

Sometimes stress and worry
can make us oversleep and
still feel tired.

YAWN!

For some people, stress and anxiety can make them
sleep too much. This is the brain's way of coping – by
switching off. If you find you are sleeping a lot but still
feel tired, grumpy and have a foggy brain, are you
worrying about something? Some worries can niggle
away in our mind without us really being aware of them,
and the brain tries to cope by shutting down. This is
obviously not a good thing when you have school and a
social life. Take some time to sit by yourself somewhere
quiet and calm, breathe deeply and see if anything
comes to mind that could be worrying you.

BODY CLOCK

You may have heard of your body clock – this is the natural rhythm of your body. It is called your circadian rhythm and is how your body deals with physical and mental processes over a 24-hour period. Your body clock affects your temperature, appetite and sleep cycles. The hormone changes that happen during puberty will affect your body clock. You may find that as you go through puberty you want to go to bed later and sleep longer in the mornings. This is quite normal but not always possible with school.

You can't ask school to start later, but there are some things you can do to help you cope with this body clock change. Try and stick to a routine, going to bed and getting up at the same time. Try not to sleep during the day (at weekends, obviously!). If you feel tired during the day, try doing some exercise. This will energise you physically, make you feel more alert and help you to sleep better later.

SERIOUS STUFF

In extreme cases, sleeping too much can be a sign of depression. If you want to sleep all the time, feel sad and withdrawn and avoid being with other people, these could be early signs that you may need to talk to a doctor about how you feel. Don't be embarrassed or ashamed to talk to your parents or carers about how you feel – depression affects people in many different ways.

WHAT'S SO GOOD ABOUT EXERCISE?

Exercise is not only good for your physical well-being but for your mental health too.

RUN HAPPY

Exercise releases chemicals into the body such as endorphins, serotonin and dopamine. These are all the body's natural painkillers that work together to make us feel good. They can actually relieve physical pain and also help to overcome mild depression, anxiety and stress. The best type of exercise to help keep your body strong and make you feel good is cardiovascular exercise. This is exercise, such as jogging, fast cycling or any sport that makes your heart pump faster and makes you feel warmer and breathe faster.

Energetic exercise also reduces the amount of cortisol hormone in your body. Cortisol is caused by feelings of stress and anxiety that can damage your body and can set up problems for your future health.

SIT HAPPY

Other types of exercise are also good for you. Yoga and stretching help to keep your body supple and help to balance your body and mind. This type of exercise can help by clearing away worries and tension and leave you feeling relaxed, calm and refreshed.

KEEP MOVING

Any form of movement is good for you. Dancing, helping with housework, cleaning the car or taking the dog for a walk are all great ways to keep your body moving. You should avoid sitting in the same position for long stretches at a time watching TV or at your computer screen. Stand up, stretch, fetch yourself a glass of water or offer to help make the tea.

"
Mum was always telling me to get off the sofa but I couldn't be bothered. I liked watching TV and being on my mobile texting mates. I used to feel sleepy all the time and felt bored and fed up. Then a friend suggested we join a local hip-hop dance group. It's brilliant. I have made loads of new friends. I feel stronger and fitter. I'm buzzing with energy the whole time and just feel so much better. It's the best thing I ever did.

Samira, 12
"

BE POSITIVE!

As we've seen, your thoughts affect how you feel mentally and physically, so try and be positive.

WHAT IS BEING POSITIVE?

Being positive is when you expect things to work out for the best. You expect to do well in the English exam and win the football match. Being positive alone won't mean you'll achieve your goals; you need to work for them as well. But if you revise for your English exam or train for a football match believing you will do your best, you are much more likely to enjoy the experience and do well than if you convince yourself you are useless at English and can't kick a football properly.

Being positive also means that if we fail, or don't do as well as we had hoped, we have the motivation to try again and do better next time. It means not being too hard on yourself when something goes wrong, accepting that you tried your best and are prepared to have another go.

ALL-ROUND BENEFITS

If you work on being positive you will feel better about yourself and your life. This will help your self-esteem and in turn good self-esteem will help you to remain positive. Being positive makes you feel happier and more fun to be around. This is great both for you and your friends and family. Being positive affects you physically too, so you might find you have more energy and enthusiasm to do stuff and try new things.

DOWN TIMES

We can't be happy, bright and smiley all the time. Everyone has some sad, disappointing and bad times and it is important to accept this. It makes us appreciate the good times all the more and means we are able to understand others who may be having a difficult time themselves. If you are going through a bad time, accept what has happened. It is good to cry and feel sad and even be angry if you need to. Talk to people you can trust about how you feel, write down your feelings, eat well, exercise and remember that whatever you are feeling will get better.

> *I always struggled with history at school but I really wanted to do well in my exams. My dad told me about visualising doing well – seeing myself succeed. I made sure I did all my revision and homework but every evening I spent 10 minutes seeing myself getting good results and thinking about how great I would feel. I passed! And I felt as good as I thought I would!*
>
> Terri, 14

A HEALTHY FUTURE

Getting into good habits now will keep you mentally and physically healthy as you grow up and become an adult.

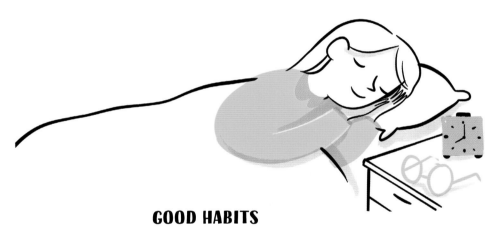

GOOD HABITS

How you treat your body now will affect it for the rest of your life. Having a balanced diet, making sure you sleep well and exercise, will help you to cope physically and mentally with school, growing up and life as an adult. If you get into good habits now, you will probably keep them forever.

BAD HABITS

It's tempting when you're young to try different things, even things that you know are bad for you. Friends can put pressure on you to smoke or drink, for example. They might say you're being pathetic or not one of them if you don't. Both smoking and drinking alcohol can severely damage your health physically and mentally and set up bad habits that you may never be able to change. Say no to smoking and drinking alcohol. Both can make you feel sick, make you smell, make your skin wrinkle and age, ruin your teeth, and will probably shorten your life. And they cost a lot of money. There really isn't a good reason to do either!

WEIGHT AWARE

More and more adults and children are obese, or very overweight. Being this overweight can damage your health now and into the future. People who are very overweight are more likely to suffer from high blood pressure, diabetes, asthma, arthritis and heart disease as an adult.

If you are worried about being overweight, speak to a trusted adult and ask to see a doctor who will give you advice about healthy eating. No matter how much you weigh don't be tempted to go on a quick-weight-loss diet. Get medical advice, find out what your ideal weight is and lose weight properly.

MENTAL IMPACT

Whatever we do to our body will affect us mentally. Smoking, drinking alcohol, and eating too much sugary, fatty food will all affect the way we feel. They can make our bodies feel sluggish, our brains foggy and can affect how the brain develops. They can affect how we think and our decision-making. For example, people are more likely to make harmful choices if they have been drinking alcohol.

THE LAST WORD – MINDFULNESS!

You might have heard this word a lot, but what is mindfulness exactly?

BEING AWARE

Mindfulness is being aware of what is happening to us, of how we are feeling physically and mentally. It is knowing what we're thinking and how we're feeling at this moment in time. Stop now and think about it. How does your body feel – tired, energized, twitchy, stiff? How do you feel – bored, interested, sad, angry? What are you thinking – what's for lunch, what am I doing later, will I see my friends tonight?

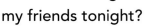

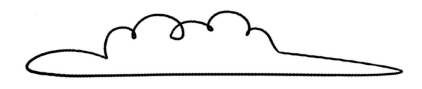

MENTAL HEALTH

By being aware of ourselves more we can notice when we feel stressed or anxious, happy or nervous. This can help us to control those feelings. For example, if you're feeling nervous about taking an exam you can start to breathe slowly and deeply to calm yourself down. Mindfulness makes us think about how we feel right now, and helps us to stop worrying about what might happen in ten minutes' time.

HOW TO BE MINDFUL

Try to become more aware of things going on around you as you walk to school, talk with friends in the playground, go shopping or have a meal with your family. Think about how you feel and how your body feels. If a negative thought comes along, face it. Say: "I feel anxious about the test." Naming your thoughts and facing them may actually make them feel less scary. Not everyone gets on with mindfulness and if it's not for you don't worry about it, at least you've tried.

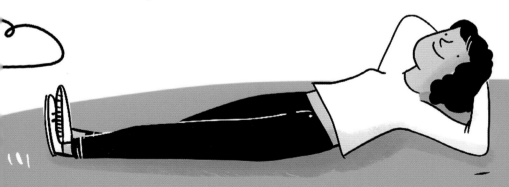

GLOSSARY

AMYGDALA
the part of your brain that affects your emotions, such as fear

ANXIOUS
nervous or worried about how something is going to turn out

ARTHRITIS
a painful disease of the joints

BINGING
doing something to excess

BODY IMAGE
how you see yourself

BRAIN STEM
the part of your brain connected to your spine

CELLS
tiny parts of the body that can only be seen with a microscope

CEREBELLUM
the part of your brain that makes your muscles work

CEREBRUM
the part of your brain that controls your thoughts and actions

CIRCADIAN RHYTHM
your natural body clock

COMPULSIVE EATING
eating lots of food in an uncontrolled way

DEHYDRATED
not having enough water

DEPRESSION
an illness that affects us physically (symptoms include not being able to sleep, always feeling tired, having no energy) and mentally (feeling anxious, tearful, hopeless and alone)

EATING DISORDERS
dangerous eating habits caused by mental health problems

EMOTIONS
feelings such as sadness, happiness, fear and anger

ENERGISED
feeling full of energy

FATAL
deadly

GROWTH SPURTS
when bones and muscles grow quickly during puberty

HEALTHY DIET
eating the right sort of
foods, avoiding too much
fast food or sugary food,
and drinking plenty of water

HORMONES
chemicals made by the
body that help it to work

ISOLATION
being alone

MENTAL HEALTH
how you feel about yourself
and the world around you,
your moods and how you
cope with life

MINDFULNESS
being aware of your
thoughts and feelings
moment by moment

MOOD SWINGS
quick changes in mood,
such as feeling happy one
minute and sad the next

NERVOUS SYSTEM
the part of your body that
controls everything you do.
It is made up of your brain,
spinal cord and nerves

NEURON
a type of cell that sends
information around the
body via chemical and
electrical signals

NUTRIENTS
substances found in food
that we need to stay healthy

OBSESS
to think about something
all the time

PITUITARY GLAND
the part of your brain that
controls your growth

POSITIVE
confident and hopeful

PUBERTY
the time when you develop
from a child into an adult

REASONING
thinking things through

SELF-ESTEEM
confidence in your own
worth and belief in yourself

STRESSED
when you feel physically or
mentally very tense
or worried

TOXIN
a poison

TRAUMA
a very distressing
experience

UNIQUE
the only one in the world

NOTES FOR TEACHERS, PARENTS AND CARERS

FOR TEACHERS

At school, teachers can encourage a healthier lifestyle by making students aware of how mind and body are linked and discussing how to establish healthy habits that will last a lifetime.

* Talk about the importance of healthy food choices and keeping well hydrated throughout the day.

* Talk about exercise and why it is important. What type of exercise do the students enjoy doing?

* Talk to students about mental health. What is good mental health? How do you get it and keep it? If a child is concerned about how they feel and their mental health, suggest they speak to their parents or carers and seek medical advice. Emphasise there is nothing to be ashamed of or embarrassed about and they are not being silly.

* Read through this book and talk in more detail about how the body and mind are closely linked.

* Talk about sleep. Why it is important? Do the students have any tips for sleeping well?

* Discuss self-esteem, what it is and why it is important. Talk about body image and the link to self-esteem.

* Talk about moods and feelings and how they can affect how you behave.

* Set 'what if' scenarios and ask the students to discuss them. For example, the difference in approaching an exam or a test with positive thinking and with negative thinking.

* Have a safe space where students can talk to a teacher about any issues they are having. Set up a noticeboard where helplines and support groups can be displayed.

FOR PARENTS AND CARERS

You are the greatest influence in your child's life. You can help them to establish habits that will keep them healthy physically and mentally for their lifetime.

* Try and have at least one family meal together, which includes plenty of vegetables to eat and water to drink, every day. Make it a 'no tech' meal, that is, no digital devices at the table.

* Encourage your child to shop and cook with you, for example by helping you to plan and prepare pizzas, salads, fillings for jacket potatoes and fruit kebabs.

* Get out together. Cycle, walk to the shops, take a stroll to the local park, play a game of football or go swimming.

* Have a picnic in the garden or local park and make sure everyone helps to prepare it.

* Don't talk about diets or become obsessed about your own weight or looks or those of other family members. Children pick up on negative comments about how skinny or fat another person is. Always be positive about your body – talk about being fit and healthy and not aspiring to look like models or celebrities.

* If you think your child is overweight, see a doctor and discuss how you can reduce your child's weight in a healthy way. Do not put your child on a fad diet or tell them they look fat. Encourage them to be fitter and healthier.

* If you think your child has an eating disorder, discuss it with your doctor or phone a helpline (see pages 46-47). Signs could be dramatic weight loss, refusing to eat proper meals or eating very little, lying about how much they've eaten, going to the loo straight after a meal and returning looking flushed, cutting food up into tiny pieces, eating a lot of food very fast, excessive exercising (every day for long periods).

* Encourage your children to help at home. Praise them when they do something well or for making an effort even if something goes wrong. Focus on their strengths and make sure they are able to learn from their mistakes.

FURTHER INFORMATION

WEBSITES AND HELPLINES

If you feel overwhelmed by any of the issues you've read about in this book, or need advice, check out a website or call a helpline and talk to someone who will understand.

www.beateatingdisorders.co.uk
Beat is a charity that says it exists to 'end the pain and suffering caused by eating disorders'. It offers help to anyone affected by an eating disorder and their loved ones.
The helpline number is 0808 801 0677.

www.childline.org.uk/info-advice/your-feelings/mental-health
Message or call the 24-hour helpline for advice or someone who'll just listen.
The helpline number is 0800 1111.

www.samaritans.org
A place where anyone can go for advice and comfort. The helpline number is 116 123.

www.sane.org/get-help
Help and support for anyone affected by mental and emotional issues.
The helpline number is 0300 304 7000.

www.supportline.org.uk
A charity giving emotional support to young people.
The helpline number is 01708 765200.

kidshealth.org/en/kids/feeling
Advice on managing emotions.

https://www.brainline.org/article/who-me-self-esteem-people-disabilities
How to boost self-esteem regardless of disabilities.

www.youngminds.org.uk
Advice for young people experiencing bullying, stress and mental or emotional anxieties.

FOR PARENTS AND CARERS

www.healthyplace.com
Information on depression and other emotional issues and advice on how to help someone going through depression.

kidshealth.org/en/parents/emotions
How to recognise an emotional phase or something more serious. Advice on how to help your child cope with emotional issues.

AUSTRALIA AND NEW ZEALAND

www.healthdirect.gov.au/partners/kids-helpline

A helpline for young people giving advice, counselling and support.
The number is 1800 55 1800.

www.kidsline.org.nz
Helpline run by specially trained young volunteers to help kids and teens deal with troubling issues and problems. The number is 0800 54 37 54.

Note to parents and teachers: every effort has been made by the Publishers to ensure that these websites are suitable for children, that they are of the highest educational value, and that they contain no inappropriate or offensive material. However, because of the nature of the Internet, it is impossible to guarantee that the contents of these sites will not be altered. We strongly advise that Internet access is supervised by a responsible adult.

BOOKS

Positively Teenage
by Nicola Morgan, Franklin Watts, 2018

The Girls' Guide to Growing Up
by Anita Naik, Wren and Rook, 2017

The Boys' Guide to Growing Up
by Phil Wilkinson, Wren and Rook, 2017

INDEX

Stalin
The Five-Year Plans
& Collectivisation

David McGill

Series editors
Nicolas Kinloch
Seán Lang

Philip Allan Updates, an imprint of Hodder Education, part of Hachette Livre UK, Market Place, Deddington, Oxfordshire OX15 0SE

Orders

Bookpoint Ltd, 130 Milton Park, Abingdon, Oxfordshire OX14 4SB
tel: 01235 827720
fax: 01235 400454
e-mail: uk.orders@bookpoint.co.uk
Lines are open 9.00 a.m.–5.00 p.m., Monday to Saturday, with a 24-hour message answering service. You can also order through the Philip Allan Updates website: www.philipallan.co.uk

© Philip Allan Updates 2008

ISBN 978-1-84489-637-0

Impression number   5   4   3   2   1

Year   2012   2011   2010   2009   2008

Printed in Spain

Hachette Livre UK's policy is to use papers that are natural, renewable and recyclable products and made from wood grown in sustainable forests. The logging and manufacturing processes are expected to conform to the environmental regulations of the country of origin.

P01240

Contents

Introduction

Stalin continues to occupy a central place in any study of twentieth-century history. As time has passed, changing contemporary preoccupations have helped to shape the way his rule is viewed. He has moved from Bolshevik conspirator to Second World War hero and then back to Cold War villain. Historians and political commentators have viewed Stalin through the prism of their own prejudices. Objectivity has been hard to come by, and it is only since the end of the Soviet Union in 1991 that scholars have been able to test many of their theories about how Stalin worked against the reality revealed by records.

Broadly speaking, there are three main approaches to Stalin. There is the critique by Cold War historians, who view him as the evil megalomaniac who warped an entire society with his own paranoid vision of Marxism. There are the countless Soviet accounts, which portray him as the great moderniser and the architect of the USSR as a superpower and victor in the 'Great Patriotic War'. Finally there are the modern revisionists, who are uncovering a more complex and perhaps morally ambiguous picture — a 'greyer' view of the Soviet Union under Stalin. They see a society where forces other than Stalin were at work, where the centre was at war with the localities and the purges spilled out of control with their own centrifugal energy.

The truth, as always, is out there somewhere, but steering a course through the conflicting views of the various historical factions can be difficult. The nature of the society being investigated adds to a student's problems. The Stalinist system was secretive and many events were not recorded. Moreover, some of the records that were made have disappeared or been lost. Stalin is still a live topic for many people, and this complicates matters — too many millions died for us to be able to view his actions with the more dispassionate gaze that distance lends.

In this book we will look first at common preconceptions of the period and of Stalin himself. In Chapter 2 we will look at Stalin's motivations for collectivisation and industrialisation and how far these were shaped by the tsarist past, Marxist ideology or personal preoccupations. In Chapters 3, 4 and 5 we will see whether collectivisation in practice bore any relation to collectivisation in theory, and whether the policy was a success or not. In Chapter 6 we will turn to industrialisation and examine Stalin's motives and methods for transforming the Soviet Union. Finally in Chapter 7 we will see how far Stalin's drive to turn the Soviet Union into a modern industrial superpower met with success.

Stalin survived until 1953, but the Second World War and the postwar period fall outside the scope of this book. The chronology of this book ends with the invasion of the Soviet Union in 1941 by Hitler's armies and the beginning of a conflict that would sorely test the nation he had fashioned in his own image, destroy the Third Reich — and also, in the eyes of some, legitimise much of Stalin's work in the 1930s.

Terms defined in the glossary are highlighted in purple the first time they appear in each chapter for easy reference.

David McGill

What are the standard views on Stalin?

Stalin was in control of the Soviet Union from 1929 to 1953, and the Communist state survived him by several decades. The focus of this book is on the first 11 or 12 years of his regime and on his attempts to modernise the USSR in order to enable it to compete with the other great powers of the age. His policies of collectivisation and industrialisation were linked. They were both launched at the same time, they ran alongside each other (and were often intertwined), and for the purpose of evaluating their degree of success or failure they are generally viewed together.

Historians' judgements of the period have been influenced by a number of factors. First, their own political sympathies have often been dominant. In the 1930s many European left-wing thinkers and politicians were keen to see the positive rather than the negative elements of the regime. During the Cold War Stalin was seen through the prism of anti-Soviet propaganda, the fear of nuclear confrontation and the Western perception of the Soviet Union as the 'Evil Empire'. Since 1991 and the end of the USSR the situation has become more complicated, with revisionist historians arguing that life in the Stalinist USSR was not as simple as it might have appeared. Historians now see that in fact competing power blocs struggled to assert themselves, and events such as the purges were not always led from the top. The opening of Soviet archives after 1991 has allowed much more detailed research to take place. It can now be seen that a number of common views favoured by historians and students might not be complete. These views are summarised under three broad headings below, although it should be noted that they sometimes overlap and interweave with each other.

Stalin was a totalitarian dictator

This view might be summarised in the statement that 'Stalin planned it all': 'all' being the power struggles, the crash process of industrialisation, and the purges.

This view is particularly popular with some Cold War historians, and is often adopted by students. It is simple, there is some truth in it, and it was certainly supported by Stalin himself. It is often the conventional student perception at GCSE and it can be summarised broadly thus. In 1924 Lenin died and there was a power struggle. The obvious favourite to succeed him was Trotsky, the brilliant Red Army leader who was a close colleague of Lenin and was popular with the young, radical members of the party. Another strong candidate was Nikolai Bukharin, a clever theoretician and supporter of the New Economic Policy (NEP) aimed at allowing the Soviet Union to industrialise gradually along loosely capitalist lines. Both candidates had supporters in the party, who broadly became known as Leftists and Rightists.

Into the ring stepped Stalin. He was a nonentity who was uninterested in anything other than personal power. Moreover, Lenin disliked him, realised he was going to become a dictator and tried to warn of this in a testament which was suppressed after his death by various self-interested members of the Politburo. Stalin now set about becoming leader. He was a member of the party's Orgburo and Secretariat, and had managed to secure control of party appointments through his role as General Secretary.

From 1924 to 1929 Stalin outmanoeuvred his enemies in a series of tactical moves. First he joined Bukharin and the Rightists against Trotsky and the Leftists and got them expelled from the party and — in Trotsky's case — from the country. Then he shifted, joining with his own supporters and radical elements in the party against the Rightists, and got them all expelled as well. By 1929 he had emerged as party leader. Now he decided to impose his order on the Soviet Union. His motivation in doing so was characteristic of a dictator. He wanted to be leader of a powerful state (he has often been compared, with some justification, with Peter the Great and Ivan the Terrible).

Next, he decided to deal with the peasants, who had been a continual obstacle since 1917. According to Marx there should be no peasants in a communist society, so the fact that they accounted for 85% of the population was somewhat inconvenient. Stalin moved against the peasants because they were withholding grain in order to inflate prices (a result of the NEP). In addition, he wanted to collectivise them because this would make them easier to control, and also because in his crude understanding of communism this would be an appropriate thing to do. Stalin launched his policy of collectivisation in mid-1929 and it was a disaster. He identified a fictitious class of 'rich' peasants called kulaks and deported or shot them as class enemies (about 10 million people in all). The peasants preferred to kill their animals rather than hand them over to the collective farms, and embarked on an orgy of slaughter that halved the Soviet Union's livestock.

Collectivisation was briefly halted in 1930 but then continued even more rapidly in the following year. Young urban activists were sent to help the OGPU force the peasants into collective farms, and a terrible wave of violence and repression swept the countryside. The Communists succeeded in collectivising the peasants, but destroyed much of the agricultural productivity of the country. Stalin also continued to export grain in order to raise capital for his industrial expansion under the Five-Year Plans. By 1932–33 there was famine in many regions of the Soviet Union. The Ukraine was the hardest-hit area, with millions dying (Robert Conquest puts the figure as high as 7 million). Soviet agricultural productivity was badly damaged, but Stalin was untroubled as long as there was grain for the cities and for sale overseas. According to some sources, he only visited the countryside a couple of times and had little understanding of what was happening there before he embarked on his policy.

At the same time, Stalin launched a crash course of industrialisation in order to catch up with the West. He realised the Soviet Union might be attacked by neighbouring capitalist countries, so decided to achieve a hundred or so years of industrialisation in ten. In one way this paid off, because later, when the Nazis invaded, Stalin's policies meant the USSR could fight them effectively, producing weapons such as the brilliant T-34 tank to defeat them. Stalin set unfeasibly high targets for Soviet industry, and through a combination of repression, bribery and propaganda he managed to achieve huge advances, even while consistently falling short of the projected figures. The Five-Year Plans succeeded in largely modernising the Soviet Union — but at a terrible cost.

From the mid-1930s, Stalin also 'purged' the Soviet Union of various enemies, both real and imagined. The kulaks were the first to go, but after murdering Kirov (the Leningrad party boss and potential rival) in 1934, Stalin targeted the Communist Party itself. He then widened the net to include anyone suspected of being an 'enemy of the people'. The purges were completed with the virtual destruction of the army's officer corps: 30,000 senior officers were arrested or shot. A by-product of this repression was the creation of a network of labour camps, often referred to as the gulag, whose inmates could be used to help fulfil the Five-Year Plans and push the Soviet Union out of the nineteenth and into the twentieth century. This period (1934–38) is known as the Great Terror.

A large-scale personality cult from 1929 onwards was aimed at brainwashing the Soviet people into revering Stalin. Historians see in the countless paintings of Stalin, doctored photographs, films and standing ovations in his honour (sometimes lasting up to half an hour) evidence supporting the idea that the people of the Soviet Union were rendered incapable of resistance to the regime.

The fact that millions lined the funeral route of Stalin (over a hundred people dying of asphyxiation in the crowds) is seen as testimony to the success of the Soviet state and of Stalin in controlling it. Soviet popular culture in this period was effectively undermined by this totalitarianism and was reduced to little more than a paean to Stalin.

Stalin had succeeded in transforming the Soviet Union into a modern state capable of fighting Nazi Germany, and when Hitler invaded in 1941 it was thanks to this modernisation that Stalin was able to defeat him. The fanatical patriotism of the Soviet people for 'Mother Russia' and Hitler's mistreatment of Soviet *Untermenschen* are additional supporting factors. In this version of events it is Stalin who occupies centre stage. It was Stalin who launched the drive for industrialisation, executed millions, led armies and also destroyed them. It is Stalin who defined the age.

There is a measure of truth in all this. Stalin did take over and refine a total-itarian system. There is no doubt that Stalin wielded a great deal of personal power and that to some degree he bore responsibility for the evils of his age. Yet this view is too simplistic. After all, the Soviet Union occupied a huge geographical area, communications were poor, and there were millions of people from different ethnic groups speaking different languages in what was essentially an empire. There was economic backwardness, isolation, and the existence of local elites and power groups with their own agendas. In short there were many other actors than Stalin on the stage and they deserve attention as well. Some of them were very important (other members of the Politburo, for example Kirov). Others played much humbler roles (the so-called kulaks or the regional party bosses who helped with collectivisation). All were involved and attempted to manipulate events and circumstances for their own benefit.

Stalin was a 'grey blur'

This is a common assumption by students and some historians. It is one of the assessments often included in source material on the dictator. It ranks alongside Trotsky's summation of him as 'one of the most eminent mediocrities in the party'. According to this viewpoint, Stalin was an uninteresting nonentity who spent his whole time as General Secretary promoting or demoting friends and enemies in order to ensure his own later rise to power. Supporters of this viewpoint argue that Stalin had no ideology or that he was too stupid to understand Marxist-Leninism. Naturally, such a view of Stalin invites specula-tion about his real motives.

Was he bad or mad? Or both, or neither? Was he acting like a traditional tsar, with the preoccupations of the ruler of a great power, or was he merely a sociopath with a penchant for personal aggrandisement? Did he believe in anything? Was he really a Marxist or Marxist-Leninist? Did he even understand what these terms meant? Did his thirst for power emerge because he was Georgian, or beaten by his father as a child? Or was he in fact a committed Communist who believed that the price paid by Soviet citizens was a necessary one to create a true Bolshevik state?

If we believe Stalin was a 'grey blur' or an 'eminent mediocrity' (and remember, these were both assessments made by his enemies), his rise to power becomes hard to understand. Some have argued that this mediocre quality was one of his strengths, allowing him to rise undetected while attention was focused on the more obvious figure of Trotsky. However, there is plenty of evidence of both his charm and his intellectual ability. Anecdotal evidence from party congresses and the Kremlin shows a man at ease with other party members, able to appeal to popular support; someone considered 'one of us' by party rank and file.

His writings on Marx and Lenin show a thorough grasp of theory. While he was no intellectual like Bukharin, and no great orator like Trotsky, his speeches on party policy show he was a committed Marxist-Leninist who understood what he was doing and believed in it. He may have been an opportunist, but he did have a set of core beliefs, and while we might find the methods he used to achieve his goals abhorrent he believed (as did many others) that they were necessary. As he stated, 'You can't make a revolution with silk gloves.'

Stalin was evil

This assessment may well be true, but it is not helpful for students to approach Stalin with this assumption fixed firmly in their minds. There is no doubt that Stalin was responsible for a large degree of suffering in the Soviet Union and that millions died under his rule. Yet to see everything that he did as stemming from some innate malice is counter-productive. As students of history we must assess Stalin in context, and in terms of many other factors that influenced what happened in Europe and the world at the time.

The assumption of Stalin's evil ignores the countless other individuals who were involved in collectivisation, the Five-Year Plans, the purges and later the war: the NKVD, the other members of the Politburo, party leaders at every level and the millions of ordinary Soviet citizens who took part in denunciations, betrayals and various other unpleasant aspects of the Stalinist Soviet Union.

Stalin did not personally supervise the whole gulag network that stretched from one end of the Soviet Union to the other. Stalin probably was 'evil', whatever definition might be attached to that word, but viewing everything that he did through this lens is likely to distort rather than clarify the study of his rule.

Any overall assessment of Stalin is in fact very difficult, and people will often arrive at a variation on the basic 'hero or villain' theme of many books and articles about him. Comparisons are made with Hitler and other dictators. Some students are fond of 'league-tabling' dictators according to how many people were killed under their regimes. Such comparisons are inevitable and can be illuminating in some areas, but the regimes these dictators led were often so different as to make the comparisons of little value. Many assessments of Stalin can be summarised as agreeing that he did terrible things and that some of his policies were failures. On the other hand, he defeated Nazi Germany, which in this view becomes a form of justification for his policies. By 1945 the Soviet Union was a superpower, and for this Stalin deserves much of the credit.

To some extent, this is how he is seen in modern Russia too. A 2003 poll by the Russian newspaper *Kommersant* asking Russians to vote for their greatest rulers put him in a respectable fourth place. Assessments of Stalin tend also to throw in some degree of crude generalisation about Russia being large and backward, unsuitable for democracy, and accustomed to having a strong man in charge. Therefore, although he is an extreme case, Stalin fits into an overall pattern of rule that mitigates some of his excesses. Proponents of this view see the Russian people as bewildered and unable to cope with anything other than repressive regimes of various sorts.

The above is a crude but not altogether inaccurate summary of this conventional view of Stalin. However, while it contains elements of truth, it blurs some of the more complex and contradictory elements of the picture. In assessing what really happened during the collectivisation process and the Five-Year Plans it is best to try to shed preconceived ideas about what Stalin wanted or did, and instead to look at what happened and why. A final assessment of the period may well prove similar to that just outlined, but it will probably be deeper and of greater complexity. In particular, when looking at Stalin and what happened from 1929 to 1939 it is important to bear in mind the uniqueness of this experience, its complexities and the difficulty of summarising it in simple terms.

Questions

1 Stalin's rule owed more to the traditions of autocracy, as practised in pre-Revolutionary Russia, than it did to either Marxist theory or Lenin's methods. Discuss this interpretation of Russian history with reference to the period 1929–53.

2 Is it fair to say that Stalin was a 'red tsar'?

3 Was Stalin the most successful of Russia's rulers in the late nineteenth and twentieth centuries? Explain with reference to the rulers of this period.

Why did Stalin industrialise the Soviet Union?

By 1929, Joseph Stalin had emerged from a protracted power struggle within the All-Union Communist Party (VKP) as undisputed leader of the nation. It had not been an easy process, as Lenin's death had left no obvious successor. On his accession Stalin launched the Soviet Union into a prolonged period of massive and unprecedented change that would transform it as much as (and some would argue more than) events after 1917 had done. This would end in the country's entering the Second World War and emerging from it as a world superpower by 1945.

This process would claim the lives of millions. Millions died of famine in the Ukraine and other regions during collectivisation and 'de-kulakisation'. Millions were rounded up in the various purges launched after 1934 and were either shot, sent to labour camps and worked to death, or exiled to remote regions of the Soviet Union. Countless others were accused of 'sabotage' or 'wrecking' during the accelerated industrialisation of the Five-Year Plans. The origins and events of the Terror are not the focus of this book, but they are inextricably linked to the events of collectivisation and the Five-Year Plans. Behind the enormous changes — peasants rounded up into collective farms and uprooted from their traditional way of life that had endured for centuries; the construction of whole new industrial cities and the superhuman labour achievements of the Stakhanovites (see Chapter 7) — lay the gulag, the NKVD and the pathological nature of Stalinism and all that it entailed.

Stalin as leader

This was a period of progress, of catastrophe and of huge suffering. The events seem so complex, the attempt to socially re-engineer an entire society and to create a new type of man so vast, and the struggles so ruthless and superhuman, that it can overwhelm the student. Few societies have ever been so relentlessly and terribly pursued by their governments into such massive change, and few societies have experienced the trauma that the Soviet Union endured between 1929 and Stalin's death in 1953. The country that emerged from these traumas was in many ways a 'modern' state and superficially seemed to have succeeded in catching up with the Western powers that had always threatened it in the past. Indeed the period of the Cold War saw the USSR outstripping the USA in some areas, and in the event of a war both sides would have had the capacity to destroy the world several times over with nuclear weapons. But the distortion of the economy and society that had been required meant that these achievements were not to last. By 1991 the Soviet regime had fallen without a shot being fired in its defence.

In the decades when communism seemed to be 'working', the titanic sacrifices demanded by Stalinism seemed to many if not excusable then at least partially justifiable by the USSR's claims to great power status. The end of the Cold War and the collapse of the USSR in 1991 have made it much harder to see Stalin's rule in a positive light. The opening of Soviet-era archives and much greater knowledge of the nature of Stalin's regime have contributed to this. Modern academics believe that many of Russia's current problems are rooted in the events of the 1930s, and in Stalin's peculiar way of attempting to solve the USSR's backwardness. Even the success of the Soviet Union in the Second World War was not necessarily due to Stalin's policies. The purging of the armed forces from 1937 and Stalin's indecision and poor tactical sense in 1941–42 almost led to Hitler's success. Some argue that it was despite, rather than because of, Stalin that the Soviet Union emerged victorious. Martin Amis wrote, 'If instead of decapitating his army, he had intelligently prepared for war, Russia might have defeated Germany in a matter of weeks.' Such a counterfactual argument is impossible to prove, but is worth considering.

Overall the legacy of Stalin's rule is now much more difficult to assess. There is the terrible nature of his totalitarian vision, with its gulag and execution chambers, which obviously invites comparison with Hitler. There is also the comparative 'success' of the Soviet model (at least for a time). The rapid industrialisation, the military defeat of Nazi Germany and the emergence of the USSR as a superpower to rival America are all seen as 'credits' as opposed to the 'debits' of those millions of dead. Hitler and Stalin, fascism and communism, have often been compared and contrasted. As models of totalitarianism, as paths to modernity, as experiments in social and national engineering, as twentieth-century phenomena, the two systems are often taught together or written about in single volumes. It is certainly helpful to compare the two regimes, but for the purposes of this book it would be more helpful to leave aside such comparisons until the end.

The Great Turn

The announcement of the First Five-Year Plan at the Fifteenth Party Congress in December 1927 marked the end of the NEP. This policy had been Lenin's response to the collapse of the economy after the Civil War, the rebellion of the sailors at Kronstadt and growing peasant hostility to the Communist Party. Essentially it had been a breathing space: a retreat from the total control of 'war communism' and a return to a degree of limited localised capitalism, with the peasants being able to sell produce at market prices. The policy had been successful in restoring a degree of prosperity and harmony to Soviet society but had not been popular with the party faithful; arguments had raged about it from the beginning. While Stalin was not yet in total control of the party by this stage, he was certainly its leading influence. The First Five-Year Plan set very high targets for industry and also contained demands for collectivisation of agriculture. Stalin had apparently decided that the grain procurement crisis of 1927–28 demanded a harsh response.

There were other motivations for collectivisation than simply securing grain and controlling the peasantry. At a wider level in the party there was a feeling that the NEP had been a 'retreat' from Marxism and that, while it had provided a breathing space for the Communist regime to recover, it was not turning the USSR into the proletarian, industrial and socialist society that had been imagined in 1917 and before. Stalin's move to the left and his support for rapid industrialisation and the Five-Year Plans were popular with party members and urban workers. His denunciations of 'specialists' and 'intellectuals' alongside his obvious contempt for the peasantry were popular in the cities, and there was significant support 'from below' for moves to radicalise the incomplete revolution and attack the final bulwarks of resistance to the new society being created.

The shift in policy that took place in late 1927 and 1928 marked a new direction for Stalin and the party. The Soviet Union moved towards a 'command economy' in which the state controlled all aspects of production and supply, setting targets and pushing the country towards a modern, urban society. The 'Great Turn' is the title given to this shift in direction. The economist Strumilin summarised the new attitude of the party to economic planning when he stated, 'Our task is not to study economics but to change it. We are bound by no laws. There are no fortresses which Bolsheviks cannot storm. The question of tempo is subject to decision by human beings.' The modernisation of the Soviet Union was as much a question of will as one of economic strategies. The idea that modernisation was a matter of collective effort and application was to find expression in the Stakhanovite campaigns of the 1930s and the continual ratcheting-up of targets and goals throughout the industrial expansion of the same period.

Stalin's move towards support for collectivisation was gradual. He had never had much time for the peasants and favoured heavy industrialisation and radical measures to bring about communism. The Civil War had succeeded in central-ising power in the hands of the Communist Party and there was little real opposition to it after 1921–22. Factional infighting had largely been resolved by 1929, with Stalin the clear 'winner' and the other leading figures who might have succeeded Lenin exiled or isolated. However, there was still much to do. Stalin clearly felt that the work begun in 1917 towards creating a new society was still incomplete. He had accepted that revolutions would not necessarily occur in other European countries and thus the Soviet Union would remain isolated. Trotsky's idea of 'permanent revolution' had been rejected, and in the absence of such upheavals in other European states Stalin had decided on a policy of 'Socialism in one country'.

In fact he had come to believe that the Soviet Union must modernise alone and thus serve as an example to Marxists in other countries struggling to overthrow the existing order. In a speech to industrial managers in 1931 he reminded them that the transformation of the Soviet Union would serve as an example to the proletariat across the globe. They would look at the USSR and declare, 'There you have my advanced detachment, my shock brigade, my working-class state, my fatherland.' The transformation of the Soviet Union would be primarily achieved by industrialisation, but to support this process the peasantry would have to be brought into line. Early in 1928 Stalin had stated, 'We cannot allow our industry to be dependent on the caprice of the kulaks.' This view was shared by many in the party who felt that the progress of the revolution was being slowed, indeed seriously threatened, by the obstructionism of the peasantry.

There was also theoretical support for this squeezing of the peasantry. Marx had argued that the bourgeoisie had accumulated the wealth necessary to launch the industrial revolution through the same process, with the addition of plenty of colonial plunder. He had called this process 'primitive capitalist accumula-tion'. Yevgeny Preobrazhensky (one of the leading party theoreticians from 1917) had argued that in the Soviet Union the same process could be achieved through a process of 'primitive socialist accumulation'. The Communist Party could manipulate prices, raise taxes, requisition grain and generally transfer resources from the private sector to the state. As the only really 'private' sector left was the peasantry, this in effect meant funding industrial expansion by exploitation of the peasants.

Bukharin had opposed this, stating that it would amount to a 'proletarian dicta-torship in a state of war with the peasantry'. He claimed with dubious accuracy that Lenin had supported the idea of an alliance between workers and peasants. He had argued for the creation of a prosperous peasantry, even going so far as to exhort them to get rich: 'Enrichez-vous.' However, the isolation of Bukharin and his supporters meant such calls for moderation were now unheeded. Indeed, another factor had been added that was to make the collectivisation process even more brutal. This was the identification of a class of rich peasants, or 'kulaks', who had to be neutralised or even destroyed in the countryside.

Imposing control

Another important factor to bear in mind (and one that may seem paradoxical) was the relative weakness of the Communist Party in the Soviet Union. While it is true that the VKP was 'totalitarian', it was also haunted by the same problems of ruling the vastness of Russia that had plagued the tsars. Lenin had succeeded in defeating the Whites and then in suppressing the peasant revolts, but on the ground the party was still weak. Huge distances separated the urban centres, and remote provinces were hard to control from the centre. Many regional party organisations were relatively autonomous, with little contact with the party headquarters in Moscow or Leningrad. Stalin had the secret police, the OGPU and later the NKVD, and the huge prison camp network in Siberia, but to some extent his use of them was an admission of failure. Recently some historians have talked of a 'civil war' within the party between the centre and the localities, between the upper echelons and the middle management. This conflict was to be resolved only by the purges of the 1930s.

The Communist Party had expanded its membership in the immediate aftermath of the revolution. Between 1917 and 1922 more than 1 million people had joined the party, but these were mostly urban workers (although many had originally come from the countryside). These 'new' Communists, having escaped from what they saw as backward and rural origins, were often the most fanatical supporters of collectivisation in later years. They wanted to urbanise the countryside, to bring in electrical power, schools and hospitals. Communism would destroy the old ways and bring in a new, rational order. The 'heroic' period of the revolution and the Civil War continued to have an appeal for this second generation of Communists, many of whom saw Stalin's Five-Year Plans and collectivisation policies as a chance to prove themselves.

The Communist Party had met with some success in its attempts to infiltrate the countryside. Its youth organisation the Komsomol grew rapidly, from

80,000 members in 1922 to more than half a million by 1925. The Komsomol tried to direct the energy of its members against the old established order in the village: the Orthodox Church and the elders. Many of its members wanted nothing more than to leave this rural world and move to the cities, as young people throughout history have done. The Red Army also attracted village youths, and it was often veterans of the Civil War who became the more radical members of the village on their return (many of them were to join the requisition squads of the collectivisation period). Yet despite making some inroads into the countryside, the party found the vast majority of peasants remained beyond its direct control.

Only 15% of rural party members were engaged in farming, and outside the townships there were few party members. The rural soviets were ineffective: as Orlando Figes notes, 'The villagers often elected a simpleton or an alcoholic, or perhaps some poor peasant in debt to the village elders, in order to sabotage the Soviet's work.' The party cut the number of soviets, which made matters worse as it left the vast majority of villages with no soviet at all. Figes notes that by 1929 the average rural soviet was trying to control up to nine villages with a population of up to 1,500. There were no telephones, and it was often impossible to collect taxes. The rural police force was tiny, with one policeman for up to 20,000 people scattered among 18–20 villages. One of the factors that helped push the Communist Party towards collectivisation, therefore, was not strength but weakness. In fact it was more than this: it was frustration. It was, as one author on collectivisation wrote, 'the rage of the state'.

Ironically, members of the Communist Party in the 1920s came to feel very much as the imperial bureaucracy had in the tsarist period: isolated in an ancient world, a dark world of superstition and unchanging ways. Party leaders, as Alexander Tsipko wrote, 'had come to find themselves in a besieged fortress…surrounded by a commodity and peasant world'. They despised the peasants, who in turn (as they had done throughout Russian history) withdrew to the village and their self-willed isolation. The peasants felt that nothing good came from the cities, from the tsar or the Communist regime: only taxes. In this summation they were right, for in fact something much worse than anything they had experienced was on its way: collectivisation. Stalin had decided in 1921–28 that this would be an effective solution to the various problems the countryside represented. First, collectivisation would break the peasantry and their backwardness, their isolation, their infuriating refusal to welcome the Communist revolution. Second, it would solve the problems of funding the Five-Year Plans. Grain would be exported to pay for industrial expansion. Finally, for Stalin there was the additional benefit that his 'de-kulakisation' drive would fill the gulag. Millions of labourers would effectively be worked to death in order to achieve rapid modernisation of the USSR.

Pinpointing the exact moment when Stalin decided to collectivise is impossible. The need to industrialise and the strong conviction of Stalin that the Soviet Union was threatened by hostile capitalist (and later Fascist) states that 'encircled' it must be seen as one of the critical motivating factors. The demands of the Five-Year Plans required capital investment, and in the absence of loans (who would lend the Soviet Union money in 1929?) that cash would have to come from the countryside. The background of state–peasant conflict from 1917 to 1922 was obviously important. The ideological nature of the Communist Party's viewpoint (which was essentially hostile to the peasants) was also critical. The weakness of the party on the ground in rural areas and its patent failure to expand its control to the villages was an essential factor in its decision effectively to 'declare war' on the countryside.

At a Central Committee meeting in July 1928 Stalin justified his imminent decision to hit the peasants hard. He stated that the Soviet Union had to squeeze the peasantry in order to build railways and hydroelectric power stations. He declared:

> England squeezed the juice out of all its colonies for hundreds of years…Germany built its industry on five billions of reparations after the Franco-Prussian war…America developed its industry by raising loans in Europe. Our country cannot, must not, go in for robbing colonies or foreign countries.

Instead the party would have to look to the peasantry as the means of raising the capital for industrialisation and providing enough food for the cities, and the only way to guarantee that was to collectivise. 'Extraordinary measures' would be necessary, Stalin announced, 'to save the country from a general economic crisis'. In 1927–28 these extraordinary measures had consisted of an enforced procurement, but Stalin wanted to go further and ensure that the state had access to all the grain it needed every year without having to send out the requisition squads.

It is important to bear in mind that collectivisation was popular with rank-and-file party members who wanted to create a modern Marxist state, and who felt that sacrifices were necessary to achieve it. Stalin certainly had little problem recruiting thousands of urban activists to support the security forces in the 1930s (the so-called 'twenty-five thousanders'). However, as the process continued and the high cost it incurred in human suffering became apparent, there was growing unease in the party leadership concerning the cost of collectivisation. Leningrad party chief Kirov was an obvious example. Some believe that growing knowledge of the reality of her husband's policies contributed to the suicide of Stalin's second wife Nadezhda in November 1932. At a wider level, however, it seems that many remained largely ignorant of the terrible cost and indeed failures of collectivisation. Yevgenia Ginzburg (author of a famous memoir, *Journey into the Whirlwind*) was 'purged' in the 1930s and spent many years in the gulag. She had been a party bureaucrat and enthusiastic supporter of collectivisation before her arrest (like many others later caught up in the Terror).

Lastly we must add Stalin to the equation. After all, he was the leader of the nation at this time. His interventions in policy were decisive, and it was above all Stalin who pushed the process through to its conclusion. Lenin compromised when faced with the blood sacrifice needed to break the peasantry. Bukharin advocated alliance and gradual change. But Stalin was ruthless and determined enough to collectivise whatever the cost and to continue the policy in the face of mounting evidence that it was a disaster. From late 1929, when collectivisation was fully revealed and endorsed by the party leadership as policy, it was Stalin who was to be its driving force.

Questions

1 What were the driving forces behind industrialisation in the USSR under Stalin?
2 Was Stalin's policy of industrialisation a pragmatic choice or was it dictated by Marxist beliefs?
3 Why did Stalin make the Great Turn?

Why collectivisation?

Collectivisation was not a new policy. The idea of the peasants giving up their private landholdings and the world of the *mir* had appealed to Bolshevik minds since before the revolution. The Communist Party was an urban party, a party of the industrial workers and the proletariat, the party of industry and the factory floor. The soviets of soldiers and workers that the party had come to dominate by October 1917 were the world it was familiar with. Party figures such as Lenin had spent the years before the revolution in exile in Geneva, Paris, London and other great cities of Europe, in countries where Marx had believed the revolution was likely to occur. Although many of the Bolsheviks had been exiled to Siberia before 1917 for varying periods and with varying degrees of success, they had little understanding of, or interest in, rural Russia.

Taming the peasants

The Bolsheviks were never popular with the peasantry. Although the peasants constituted some 80% of the population, their support for the Bolsheviks remained fractional. The party of the peasants was the Socialist Revolutionaries (the SRs). By 1917 the SRs had compiled a list of some 242 peasant manifestoes asking for even distribution of land among the peasants, alongside other measures that had attracted their support. Lenin had incorporated some of these demands into the Bolshevik programme in August 1917, stating:

> The peasants want to keep their small farms, to set equal standards for all, and to make readjustments on an egalitarian basis from time to time. Fine. No sensible socialist will differ with the peasant poor over this…The crux of the matter lies in political power passing into the hands of the proletariat.

However, it is clear that Lenin's support for such policies was opportunistic. In reality he wanted to incorporate the peasantry into the Communist state and had in mind some form of eventual collectivisation. In fact the policy should be seen in the context of a long-running conflict between the Communist Party and the peasantry that can be traced right back to this false compromise of 1917 and the Civil War that followed. The real crux of the matter was that Lenin and his supporters were never really interested in meeting peasant demands. He needed to ensure their support, or at least their acquiescence in the initial takeover of power, but there is little indication that he understood their problems or was even particularly interested in doing so. Ilya Shkapa wrote, 'Lenin had agreed to the programme of the Socialist Revolutionaries to socialise the land, but the programme of the Bolsheviks was in favour of nationalising the land.' Lenin's agreement with the SRs in 1917 and the land decrees that followed were purely tactical. Lenin himself said:

> We Bolsheviks were opposed to the law…Yet we signed it, because we did not want to oppose the will of the majority of the peasants…We did not want to impose on the peasants the idea that the equal division of land was useless, an idea which was alien to them. Far better, we thought, if, by their own experience and suffering, the peasants themselves came to realise that equal division was nonsense…That is why we helped to divide the land, although we realised it was no solution.

So from the start there was tension and dissimulation between Lenin and the SRs (and thus their peasant supporters). Once they had seized power in October 1917 the Bolsheviks moved quickly to silence opposition. The Constituent Assembly was closed down after one day and the SRs (who had won 410 seats compared with the Bolsheviks' 175) were quickly suppressed. Lenin conveniently argued that his Soviet government represented a higher stage of democracy than an elected assembly, and so the first properly elected body in Russian history was dissolved. Indeed some of the SRs ended up joining the 'White' armies in the Civil War that followed, while peasant groups formed independent 'Green' armies that fought both Bolshevik forces and their enemies.

The Civil War brought terrible suffering to the peasants. The fighting between the Red armies of the Communist Party and the White armies of their various enemies generally brought only misery to the peasant communities they ransacked and pillaged on their campaigns. The Communist Party enjoyed marginally more support among the peasants thanks to its land reforms of 1917–18 and the knowledge that if the Whites won, the result would be a return to some form of tsarism and the loss of any hope of change. However, the demands of war communism, with the requisitioning of grain and the conscription of men into the Red armies, meant that by 1920 revolts against the Communist Party were spreading. The demands of the Communist Party remained relentless and caused widespread suffering. Why were the Communist Party leaders so uninterested in helping the peasantry?

Orlando Figes argues:

> The Bolsheviks' civil war against the countryside was rooted in a fundamental mistrust — bordering on hatred — of the peasantry. As Marxists they had always viewed the peasantry with something akin to contempt…the peasants were too illiterate and superstitious, too closely tied to the Old Russia, to play a role in the building of their new society.

Alan Bullock agrees with this view. He states:

> The unique feature of Russian society was the size of its peasant population…The Bolsheviks/Communists had never been able to come to terms with this phenomenon, which had no place in the Marxist schema. They resented their dependence on this huge rural sector…they saw it as the source of Russia's backwardness.

Martin Amis summarises thus:

> In Bolshevik terms the peasantry was (as psychologists say when referring to a huge and unmentionable family dysfunction) 'the elephant in the living room'. The peasantry, in the Marxist universe, wasn't really meant to be there. In the Marxist universe Russia was supposed to be more like Germany or France or England, with their well-developed urban proletariats. Yet the Russian peasants were intransigently actual: they comprised 85% of the population. And as landholders they were technically bourgeoisie, technically capitalist.

Alexander Tsipko, a Soviet academic, summed up the problem when he wrote that the Marxist approach caused 'monstrous strain in a country where 80% of the population were seen as an obstacle on the path to an ideal society'. Thus it was that although they had largely defeated their White enemies by 1921, the Red armies struggled to defeat the widespread peasant insurgency of the same year. Rebel peasant armies had seized control of large areas of the Soviet Union and Soviet power in much of the countryside was almost non-existent. A rash of workers' strikes in the cities also threatened the Communist Party with defeat. Lenin mobilised all his forces for one final onslaught to consolidate his regime. The revolts in the cities were crushed (with the suppression of the Kronstadt rebellion in March marking the final phase of this action). The party then turned to the countryside. The spring of 1921 saw massive military campaigns against the peasant rebels. In Tambov province more than 100,000 soldiers occupied the region, and planes, poison gas and concentration camps were all deployed to defeat the rebels. By the late summer of 1921 most of the peasant armies had been defeated, and famine finished off any last sparks of resistance.

The Volga famine of 1921–22 is reckoned to have killed some 5 million people. It has been estimated that by the spring of 1921 up to one quarter of the peasantry in the Soviet Union was starving. The refusal of the Soviet government to admit the scale of the problem caused many deaths, although a relief effort was finally allowed. Spearheaded by the American Relief Agency (ARA) (which at the height of the operation in the summer of 1922 was feeding more than 10 million people a day), the famine relief was a success and allowed the countryside a breathing space, so that by 1922–23 agriculture had largely recovered. In fact, that year saw bumper harvests, but it was no thanks to the Communists that the dire crisis had been averted. Lenin had tried to obstruct the operation at all stages and continued to export cereals in this period. The

Americans were so alienated by his approach that public support in the USA rapidly dried up. By the summer of 1923 the ARA suspended its operations and Lenin subsequently imprisoned many of the Russians involved in administering the relief. He even went so far as to advise Maxim Gorky (the famous author who had mobilised international aid) to take a holiday, 'for the sake of his health'.

Lenin's adoption of the NEP, like his adoption of SR demands in 1917, can be seen as a purely tactical ploy to ensure his own survival. He realised that unless he compromised again with the peasantry, the Communist Party would be destroyed. Once again the Communist Party was forced to deviate from its planned march to the Marxist utopia by the tiresome demands of the peasants, and so the years from 1924 to 1928 should be seen as a respite, before renewed action against the obstructive rural mass that hindered the modernisation of the country. Orlando Figes summarises this succinctly:

> The events of 1918–21 had left a deep scar on peasant–state relations. Although the civil war had come to an end, the two sides faced each other with deep suspicion and mistrust during the uneasy truce of the 1920s. Through passive resistance and everyday forms of resistance — foot dragging, habitual failure to understand instructions, apathy and inertia — the peasants hoped to keep the Bolsheviks at bay…Militant Bolsheviks were increasingly afraid that the revolution would degenerate, that it would sink in the 'kulak' mud, unless a new civil war was launched to subjugate the village to the town.

This, then, was the context of collectivisation: a long-running war between the Communist Party and the peasantry, the roots of which can be traced back to 1917. The events of 1918–21 had essentially resulted in victory for neither side, both sides exhausted by the struggle and the Bolsheviks by their drive to consolidate their rule. However, in the ferocity of its campaigns against the peasant rebels, its indifference to peasant suffering and famine and the incomprehension with which it viewed the world of the village, the Communist Party in its early years was behaving similarly to the way in which it would in the era of collectivisation. The difference was that for Stalin there would be no pause or halt: the peasants would be subjugated, whatever the cost.

It is also worth bearing in mind that for the Soviet Union to modernise, the peasantry would have to be absorbed into a predominantly urban, literate society. Whether this was a gradual or rapid process, at some stage they would have to adapt to a new type of life. This does not excuse the suffering caused by the speed and violence of the Stalinist process, but it does put it into some kind of context. Chris Ward writes:

> Industrialisation — in any country and under any political or social system — involves more or less rapid urbanisation and the growth of populations no longer able to feed

themselves.... Set in the frame of world history since the eighteenth century, Stalin's agrarian revolution is noteworthy only for the scale and speed of its implementation, and the compression of the misery involved into an extraordinarily short timescale.

The party background, 1921–29

The run-up to collectivisation can be a confusing period for students. There was a background of Bolshevik hostility towards the peasantry stretching back to 1917. The failure of war communism had been followed by compromise. Lenin had effectively called a ceasefire with the introduction of the NEP. The NEP had been successful in restoring a measure of normality to the Soviet economy and had improved relations with the peasants. Yet the Communists still viewed the peasants with suspicion, and vice versa. There were a number of reasons for this: the problems with fitting the peasants into a Marxist schema, the traditional backwardness and isolation of the peasants, the brutality of the fighting in the Civil War and the famine that followed. Relations were therefore soured from the start, and the central problem that the peasants presented to the party was still apparent. What should the party do?

The NEP was not an ideal Communist solution to the problems posed by the peasantry. Allowing them to trade grain and food in a semi-capitalist fashion would not work in the long term. How could the Soviet Union become Communist if more than 80% of its citizens effectively operated in a capitalist limbo? The Communist Party might retain control of the commanding heights of the economy with its state factories, but if the peasants remained outside the system and retained their almost feudal existence, how could the Soviet Union really modernise and move forward? This issue bothered many in the party, and the NEP never really gained mass support among the rank and file of the Communist Party. Trotsky and others on the party's Left were very critical of the policy. Bukharin and others on the party's Right supported it. They believed change should be gradual and moderate and that the peasants could be allies of the regime if given time. Stalin appeared to support Bukharin and opposed the Left.

This conflict had rumbled on from 1924 to 1928 without being resolved. Trotsky was initially the main opposition figure. He wanted more radical measures to be taken, and criticised the party's direction. He was, however, isolated at this stage and by 1925 had retreated from the public debate after being attacked violently by various party members. From 1923 to 1927 the Left Opposition emerged, led by some influential Old Bolsheviks, including Zinoviev (head of the party in Leningrad) and Kamenev (head of the party in Moscow). They criticised the NEP and called for the party to support heavy industrialisation and grain procurements. A party agreement to ban 'factionalism' in 1921 hindered effective debate, as those calling for change could be labelled 'wreckers' and dismissed. Stalin had supported Bukharin and others in opposing the Left Opposition. He stated his support for the NEP and 'gradualism' and appeared to be a moderating force between the two factions. At this stage the majority of the party seemed to be broadly in favour of moderation, although they were uneasy about the NEP. At the Fourteenth Party Congress in 1925 discussion over the NEP had become heated and Kamenev had attacked Stalin publicly. Bukharin too had been targeted by the Left Opposition and Stalin had offered him public backing.

Stalin at this stage cast himself successfully in the role of a 'moderate'. He appeared to those in the party as a mediator, a man who wanted to avoid sudden and radical change, a gradualist who wanted to consolidate the rule of the Bolsheviks after the terrible years of the Civil War and the Red Terror. He also successfully appealed to younger elements of the party as 'one of them', someone who spoke for them against the functionaries who appeared to dominate the party. Ruth Fischer describes him at the Fifth World Congress of Communist Parties, held in Moscow in June 1924:

> Smoking his pipe, wearing the characteristic tunic and Wellington boots, he spoke softly and politely with small groups, presenting himself as the new type of Russian leader. The younger delegates were impressed by the revolutionary who despised revolutionary rhetoric, the down to earth organiser whose quick decisions and modernised methods would solve the problems in a changed world.

Stalin's other talent was organisational. One of his most famous slogans in 1933 was 'personnel decides everything', and this was as true a decade earlier. From 4 April 1922 he was General Secretary of the party, which gave him a large degree of control over appointments. The party's Central Committee became his main instrument of power. He promoted Vyacheslav Molotov and Valerian Kuibyshev to be his fellow secretaries (both men would remain loyal supporters in the decades to come). Another close ally was Lazar Kaganovich, who took over the party's organising and distributing section. This section decided who would attend party congresses and which members were posted where. Stalin was also a member of the Politburo and of the smaller Orgburo (which decided which Politburo resolutions would be adopted). In addition he controlled the Workers' and Peasants' Inspectorate, which reviewed all government decisions, and ran the Commissariat of National Minorities, which had made the USSR a centralised empire rather than a federal state. Stalin had worked with the OGPU to crush dissent in various regions, notably his native Georgia (where he was aided by another of his later cronies, Sergo Ordzhonikidze). The Communist Party justified this continuation of what Lenin had called the 'prison of the peoples' with typical self-confidence. Zinoviev stated in 1919, 'We cannot do without

Azerbaijan's oil or Turkestan's cotton. We take these things which we need, but not in the way the old exploiters took them, but as elder brothers who are carrying the torch of civilisation.' Lastly Stalin dominated the Comintern. No wonder that Lenin, in his final testament, had warned about Stalin concentrating so much power in his hands.

In addition to this, Stalin forged increasingly strong links with the *Cheka* and later its successor bodies the GPU and the OGPU. During the Civil War Stalin's role had been primarily organisational: resolving supply problems and supporting the Red Army and the *Cheka* in the rear zones. Stalin became close to the head of the *Cheka*, a sinister character called Feliks Dzerzhinsky. By 1922 he effectively controlled a paramilitary organisation that numbered some half a million. The Civil War had seen the *Cheka* execute tens of thousands of its enemies and send many more to concentration camps. It had also supported the party's economic policies with the use of force, and prisoners taken forfeited their property to the *Cheka*. Initially Dzerzhinsky had worked closely with Trotsky, but they had deepening disagreements and the head of the *Cheka* increasingly sided with Stalin. In 1922 the *Cheka* was formally abolished and replaced by the GPU (State Political Directorate), which was now answerable to the Ministry of the Interior. It seemed that an end to the repression of the Civil War was in sight. Execution figures also fell, from a high of 9,701 in 1920 to 414 in 1923 (official figures: the reality, particularly in 1920, would have been far higher). Dzerzhinsky remained head of the GPU and his alliance with Stalin remained intact. In 1924 Dzerzhinsky aided Stalin in making sure Trotsky was away for Lenin's funeral while Stalin laid the groundwork for securing his position as primary heir to Lenin. In 1926 Dzerzhinsky died and was replaced by Vyacheslav Menzhinsky. Menzhinsky too was to be crucial in Stalin's struggle for power and later in pushing through collectivisation by putting the full state apparatus of terror at his disposal.

From 1925 to 1927 Zinoviev and Kamenev were effectively isolated. They lost their jobs as party leaders in their respective cities, and although they retained their place in the Politburo they found themselves outnumbered. Too late they allied with Trotsky and agreed to bury old resentments, forming a 'United Opposition' against Stalin and other party leaders. This United Opposition challenged Stalin at a Central Committee plenum in July 1926. They tried to persuade the other party members that Stalin and Bukharin were taking the party the wrong way and that the revolution of 1917 was being betrayed, but they were too late. Their earlier quarrelling and the time it had taken them to organise cost them dearly. Stalin was prepared: the various committees, meetings and bodies such as the party Congress and the Comintern were already stuffed with Stalin's supporters. Zinoviev was expelled from the Politburo.

Attempts by the three to 'go public' in September 1926 and organise mass meetings failed, and led to Trotsky and Kamenev losing their seats in the Politburo. Zinoviev also lost his place on the Comintern Committee. At the party conference that year all failed to get the fair hearing they had hoped for. Throughout late 1926 and into 1927 public attacks on them grew, and Stalin headed attempts to strip them of any remaining party posts and power. Demonstrations in support of them were broken up by police and OGPU agents and some dissident Bolsheviks were arrested. Trotsky, Zinoviev and Kamenev were all expelled from the party. At the Fifteenth Congress in December 1927, 75 of their supporters and 18 Democratic Centralists were stripped of party membership. The move against the Left Opposition had been successful. Stalin had triumphed. Nikita Khrushchev, a delegate at the Congress and head of the Soviet Union after Stalin, remembered his support for the move: 'At that time we had no doubt Stalin and his supporters were right…we realised that a merciless struggle against the Opposition was inevitable…When you chop down a forest, the wood-chips fly.'

Pragmatist or ideologue?

However, any expectation that the removal of the United Opposition would bring a period of tranquillity was soon abandoned. No sooner had Stalin forced the expulsion of this group than he began to fall out with those gradualists and Rightists that he had hitherto supported. This is why it is difficult for historians to work out exactly what Stalin believed in. From 1921 to 1927 he supported Bukharin, the NEP and generally moderate policies. He led the attacks on Trotsky, Zinoviev and Kamenev and publicly denounced their policies. But as soon as he had got rid of them he began to change his direction, eventually putting many of their ideas into practice. Many historians present this shift as a strategy adopted by Stalin so that he could become supreme leader of the Soviet Union. Conventional wisdom has it that his adoption of different ideologies was opportunistic and concerned only with destroying his enemies and emerging as the sole power. Historians who support this view depict Stalin as a schemer who changed sides in order to destroy any opposition. Initially he opposed the Left in order to neutralise Trotsky, the main threat to his leadership. Once he had achieved this he moved against the Right (led by Bukharin), before achieving total power in 1929. Stalin now combined the posts of General Secretary and Premier. Moreover he had removed any effective opposition and was finally in a position to decide policy and act as he saw fit. How deeply his beliefs were held is debatable. Some see Stalin as essentially a pragmatist, while others view him as an ideologue.

Certainly Stalin could be pragmatic, capable of flexibility under duress. For example, during the Second World War he unashamedly expropriated elements of Russia's tsarist past to harness support for the war effort. However, Stalin was also an ideologue, and his grasp of Marxist theory, although not as thorough as Bukharin's or Lenin's, was adequate. A series of lectures given by Stalin in January 1924 after Lenin's death and published as *Foundations of Leninism* show he had grasped the fundamentals. It was a book that was to prove popular with ordinary party members and began to establish him as a 'man of the people'. Above all, he emphasised party unity, a stance that was to pay dividends in the 1920s as he labelled his various enemies as 'factionalists'. Stalin at this stage also had the advantage of his plebeian background. He was keen to portray himself as a man who understood where the wider party membership came from. He stated, 'We Communists are people of a special mould…the sons of the working class, the sons of want and struggle, the sons of incredible privation.' His control of party appointments allowed him to advance those he liked and who he felt would support him. He generally preferred members from working-class back-grounds and to some extent proletarianised the party.

In discussion he appeared to put the interests of the party first. Boris Bazhanov worked with Stalin at the time and wrote, 'At meetings Stalin never took part in a discussion until it was ended. Then when all had spoken, he would get up and say in a few words what was in effect the opinion of the majority.' In public meetings he attacked any deviation from the party line and came to be seen as a champion of party unity. This allowed him to attack Trotsky, whose views in 1923–24 were definitely not shared by the majority of party members. It also allowed him to isolate Zinoviev and Kamenev. From 1927 this image allowed him to shift back to the left and begin to distance himself from Bukharin and the Right. How much of this shift was tactical and how much was ideological it is difficult to say, but it seems safe to conclude that Stalin was genuinely on the left of the Bolshevik Party, and once Trotsky and his supporters had been eliminated it was inevitable that he would drift back towards their policies.

By January 1928, with Trotsky exiled, first to Central Asia and then in 1929 to Turkey, Stalin was free to realign himself with more radical factions of the party. In his struggle with the Left Opposition he had relied on support in the Politburo and Central Committee from Nikolai Bukharin and his supporters. Bukharin was a popular member of the party who had moved from a radical stance in the Civil War to a moderate position afterwards. He supported the NEP, gradual industrialisation and accommodation with the peasantry. His circle included Nikolai Uglanov, the trade unionist Mikhail Tomsky and the premier, Alexei Rykov. They shared a belief in a stable society and opposed more radical elements within the party who wanted to force rapid change. Stalin had been happy with their support in his battle against Trotsky but he seems never to have been particularly happy with their overall policy in the long term. In 1925 he quarrelled with Bukharin over the NEP and began to favour rapid industrialisation. He had avoided supporting Trotsky but appears to have shared some of his ideas, albeit to a lesser degree. If Stalin was serious about upping the tempo of industrialisation, the capital for this would have to be found, and it is in this period from 1925 to 1928 that Stalin seems to have begun to focus on the peasantry and on extracting a surplus from them.

It was thus a combination of a natural tendency to radical solutions, a desire to expand his own power, and a genuine belief that the NEP had had its day and that the time had come for more rapid industrialisation that motivated Stalin in his shift away from Bukharin and to the left from 1927. Within the party, opinion was divided. Some were alarmed by the change in policy and were wary of ending the NEP and returning to what was effectively war communism. Splits began to become apparent. Bukharin, Rykov and Tomsky tried to organise opposition to Stalin, but his control of the party apparatus was too strong. He argued that the NEP should adapt and move to the left, and blamed kulak sabotage and opposition for rural problems. At the July 1927 plenum this division began to become obvious, with Bukharin heckled and interrupted while he tried to state the arguments for moderation. However, Stalin was prepared to bide his time. He needed to make sure that Trotsky and his supporters were properly eliminated before moving against Bukharin and his associates. Bukharin tried to organise an effective opposition; he met up with the expelled Kamenev to warn him and to try to enlist his support. He was worried Stalin was preparing to swing to the left and adopt the very policies he had himself attacked the year before (those of the so-called United Opposition, led by Trotsky).

He was right to be worried. Tensions were rising. March 1928 saw the opening of the first of the 'show trials'. The accused were technical workers and managers at the Shakhty mines in the Donets Basin. They were charged with conspiring with 'foreign powers' to sabotage the mines. Fifty-five people were charged; some even confessed. Eleven were sentenced to death and five executed. Stalin stated, 'We have internal enemies. We have external enemies. This, comrades, must not be forgotten for a single moment.' The climate in the Soviet Union was rapidly cooling. Debate was being stifled, opposition becoming redefined as treason, and the hunt was on for 'enemies' to be identified and neutralised. Collectivisation and the debate around it were becoming increasingly dangerous issues to discuss. Stalin was moving towards making his final decision and ensuring that opposition was isolated and ineffective. Throughout 1928 signals began to sound that a shift was in the air.

In May 1928 a report presented to the State Planning Commission (Gosplan) by the Supreme Economic Council called for an increase of 130% in industry in 5 years. This was to be the start of the first of the Five-Year Plans. At the Sixth World Congress of the Comintern (mid-July to September) Stalin criticised Bukharin's speech and called for a move to the left. Stalin attacked 'right deviation' abroad and demanded foreign parties purge themselves. Stalin's supporters at home began to apply the label to Bukharin and his allies, and although the Politburo appeared united in public it was obvious from this moment that splits were becoming wider beneath the surface. Stalin was preparing to put his whole weight behind a shift to the left and to support for collectivisation and heavy industrialisation. Throughout 1928 and into 1929 debates on this issue intensified.

In September 1928 Bukharin published an article, 'Notes of an Economist', that challenged the demands for heavy industry to be accelerated. He believed such an action could cause chaos. Bukharin was reprimanded by the Politburo for this but Stalin convinced him that he was prepared to compromise. In November 1928 the Politburo was still presenting a unified face to the wider party, and disagreement remained secret. However, from November 1928 onwards Stalin grew increasingly confident. At the Trade Union Congress in December 1928 Stalin called for the expulsion of 'rightists'. Bukharin was charged with opposition to the party line at a joint meeting of the Politburo and the Presidium of the Control Commission. At the Central Committee plenum in April 1928 Stalin renewed the offensive and dismissed his friendship with Bukharin: 'We are not a family circle or a coterie of personal friends; we are the political party of the working class.' Stalin's speech, 'On the Right Deviation in the CSPU', was a detailed and comprehensive attack on Bukharin and his remaining supporters. After the plenum, Bukharin and Tomsky lost their posts with the party newspaper *Pravda*, the Comintern and the trade unions.

The plenum also supported Stalin's calls for an increase in industrial output and the initiation of the Five-Year Plan. From August 1929 the campaign against Bukharin gathered force, with the publication of hundreds of articles attacking him. In November 1929 Bukharin was expelled from the Politburo. In December 1929 Stalin's fiftieth birthday was celebrated in *Pravda*. In its list of Politburo members the newspaper abandoned the practice of listing members alphabetically as an indication of the collective leadership of the party and instead distinguished Stalin as 'Lenin's first pupil' and the party's guide. Stalin had emerged as the new leader of the USSR, successor to Lenin and head of a totalitarian one-party state.

Defined opposition groups on the left and right of the party had been effectively eliminated. From this point on Stalin had a free hand to institute the policies that he wanted.

What did he want? He had accused Bukharin and his allies of being 'witch-doctors' prior to their expulsion from the party and had stated, 'Not one of you understood Lenin.' Now he was to get his chance to show the world how to create a Communist society and he felt that time was short. In *Pravda* in 1931 he wrote:

> To lower the tempo of industrialisation means falling behind, and those who fall behind get beaten…The history of old Russia consisted, among other things, in her being beaten continually for her backwardness. She was beaten by the Mongol khans. She was beaten by the Turkish beys…She was beaten by the Polish and Lithuanian gentry. She was beaten by the Anglo-French capitalists. She was beaten by the Japanese barons. She was beaten by all of them because of her backwardness, her military back-wardness, cultural backwardness, political backwardness, industrial backwardness, agri-cultural backwardness…We are fifty or a hundred years behind the advanced countries. We must make good this distance in ten years. Either we do it, or we shall be crushed.

Making 100 years of progress in a decade was clearly not going to be easy. Stalin believed that it was up to him to drag the Soviet Union into the twentieth century. The first step on the path to a successful socialist society was to incorporate the peasants into the mainstream of both society and the economy and to end their autonomy. Then their grain surplus could be used to drive industrialisation. This was not a new tactic: Witte, Russia's finance minister in the 1890s, had squeezed the peasantry to pay for industry. Then it had raised capital and also led to famine and a revival of opposition to the tsar. Stolypin (Nicholas II's prime minister) had attempted to encourage the peasants to modernise by loans and the creation of a land-bank. He had tried to undermine the power of the *mir* (the village) and its hold on the peasants and create a prosperous class of capitalist farmers whose excess wealth could kick-start a rural revolution in spending and investment. His plans, as he himself had stated, needed time ('at least 20 years of peace'). The First World War and the ensuing Civil War had destroyed much of the progress made prior to 1914 and plunged the peasantry back into famine. The NEP had bought a breathing space and allowed some recovery but now a new wave of change was about to be unleashed. Stalin was determined that nothing would stop him and that this time there would be no compromise.

Questions

1 Was the NEP working by the end of the 1920s?
2 How far was Stalin's viewpoint of the peasants influenced by Marxist beliefs and how far by experiences since 1917?
3 Why did Stalin decide collectivisation was the right policy for the USSR?

What did collectivisation mean in reality?

The complex political background of debate and conflict within the Bolshevik Party in the USSR at this time helps to make clear why Stalin embarked on the policy of collectivisation. Arguments had focused on the direction the Soviet Union would take after the Civil War and Lenin's death. Would other European countries become Communist? If not, then what did this mean for Marxism? Should the Soviet Union isolate itself and build 'Socialism in One Country'? If it decided to do so, how should it industrialise and modernise? Would the country be left alone by other European powers? Would opposition within the Soviet Union ally with opposition outside the country (as in the Civil War)? Who would lead the Soviet Union, and should the government be collective or individual? How should the USSR pay for industrialisation? What should be done with the peasants? These questions gave rise to huge debate and division within the party and the country. By the end of 1929 some of them had been resolved.

Socialism in one country

Stalin was now the undisputed leader of the USSR. He was committed to building 'Socialism in One Country' and it was an accepted fact that the Soviet Union was isolated and facing potentially hostile powers on all sides. It was also clear that the NEP was not really working in the regime's favour. Grain shortages in 1927 and 1928 seemed to indicate that peasants were either hoarding grain or growing less. Either was bad news for the leadership. Pressure was growing to make critical decisions, and many favoured increasing radicalisation. There was a sense of unfinished business. Workers in the cities, party members and leaders began to call for an increase in the tempo of revolution. Stalin sensed this. In many ways he was sympathetic to it and he was happy to force this change on a rural population that he suspected of being less than fully committed to the Communist ideals. Added to this was his natural desire to increase the Soviet Union's power (whatever else he was, Stalin was a committed nationalist) and his worry that external enemies threatened the fragile state of the nation. Radical measures were necessary and they needed to be initiated as soon as possible. There was plenty of support for this approach in the party. Abdurakhman Avtorkhanov (a graduate student at the time) recalled, 'I, of course, was on Stalin's side, because I thought…well, Lenin himself said that NEP was a pause. And so Stalin said, "The pause has finished, and we are returning to socialism and communism."'

This 'return' to socialism and communism would initially involve collectivisation allied with industrialisation. The Five-Year Plans would transform the Soviet economy, but it would be necessary to force the peasants to change, and to control their freedom to dispose of their grain. Once the peasants were under party control, the success of the Five-Year Plans would be assured. It was, however, going to be harder to persuade them of the merits of this scheme than the party leadership first thought. To some extent the period from 1929 through to the mid-1930s can be seen as a period of intense and desperate conflict between the government and a significant proportion of its subjects.

So how did collectivisation occur? What did it mean in reality? First, collectivisation was clearly linked to industrialisation. Both were part of what British historian Richard Overy calls the 'great utopian experiment…in which class was finally destroyed as a social category, to be replaced by a community based on heroic socialist construction'. Experiment is really the best word for it, as Stalin and the VKP leadership effectively embarked on a programme of massive social change without much idea of what it would mean in reality. How would collective farms work? How would peasants be paid and land allocated? How would machinery be controlled? These matters were all essentially left vague before the policy was actually launched. This lack of effective planning and a clear idea of what collectivisation would mean would lead to many disasters and millions of deaths. The philosopher Leszek Kolakowski called it 'probably the most massive warlike operation ever conducted by a state against its own citizens'.

The aim of collectivisation was to force the peasants to move to farms owned equally by all their members. These collective farms were to be run cooperatively and would be obliged to hand over a certain amount of produce to the state every year. There would be no more NEP. There would be no more individual farms and no more individual farmers selling their produce independently. Stalin still faced the challenge that Lenin had confronted, which was how to get the grain out of the countryside when there was no clear incentive to do so. Whereas Lenin had compromised in the face of wholesale peasant opposition,

Stalin had decided that such appeasement could no longer be justified. To support this switch in tactics he identified a 'kulak' class of rich peasants who were hoarding grain and opposing the regime. This class of peasants, labelled 'blood-suckers grown rich on the want suffered by the people' by Lenin, were trying to defeat the Communist revolution and needed to be destroyed. Stalin therefore allied the twin actions of collectivisation and the destruction of the kulaks into a single policy. One could not be achieved without the other. Collectivisation would involve the elimination of millions of peasants identified by Stalin as kulaks.

This threw up a very salient problem. Who were these kulaks? Identifying them was obviously crucial, as they were the group that was supposedly responsible for hoarding grain, opposing the VKP and generally undermining any chance of a successful transition to the Communist utopia envisaged by Marx and Lenin. Unfortunately for Stalin (and more so for those deemed to be kulaks), there was little agreement on how to identify this kulak class. Stalin was vague on the subject. He was unclear about what actually constituted a kulak but was certain that they were hostile and needed to be eliminated. As the pressure to collectivise was stepped up, so was the pressure to identify the kulaks and then get rid of them. The process started gradually. Collectivisation was discussed throughout 1927, and in December at the Fifteenth Party Congress Stalin appeared to have accepted a compromise with Bukharin and more moderate elements within the party. They stated that they would support collectivisation as long as it was gradual and voluntary. However, once the Congress had finished, Stalin persuaded the Central Committee (with the agreement of Bukharin, Rykov and Tomsky) to send out a number of directives ordering 'extraordinary measures' to secure grain that year. Moreover the directives threatened local party leaders with unspecified penalties if they failed to secure this grain.

Thus the stage was set for growing conflict between the centre and the localities. The party leadership was demanding increased grain procurement and collectivisation and it was up to the local parties to conform. While the purges and terror of the mid-1930s were not anticipated at this stage, it was clear that failure would bring some kind of sanction. As the pressures from the centre grew, the localities responded. These directives sparked the beginning of the collectivisation process. Local party leaders drafted in thousands of volunteers to help with procurements. Stalin and Molotov visited Western Siberia in January 1928 and spent 3 weeks touring the agricultural regions in the province. Stalin was harsh in his criticism of local leaders and pushed them to use force in getting grain out of the peasants. He wanted the poorer peasants to inform against their kulak neighbours and offered them the incentive of cheap grain confiscated from this group. Anyone opposing this could be prosecuted as a 'speculator' under Article 107 of the Criminal Code. Stalin stated, 'The Soviet government was not going to stand by and let the kulaks hold the country to ransom: there will be shortage of grain procurements as long as the kulak exists.' Roadblocks were set up and requisition squads sent out: these actions and threats of more repression to follow all succeeded in raising procurements. Stalin decided that such measures should be extended across the Soviet Union, and the success of the Urals-Siberian method, as his exercise of power in 1927 came to be known, convinced him that the peasants were an obstructive force that needed to be brought under the state's control. The same year, 1927, also saw a war-scare. Threats from Poland and deteriorating relations with the Western powers convinced Stalin that he needed to shore up the Soviet state and prepare it for potential conflict.

Stalin's increased pressure in the countryside produced a negative consequence, as many peasants sowed less for the following year, and some sold their farms altogether. The drive to step up the pace of collectivisation also increased the impetus to eliminate the kulak class, who would (Stalin believed) oppose and 'wreck' the transition. But where was this amorphous and hostile group? Did it even exist? In 1926, A. P. Smirnov, the Commissar for Agriculture, had distinguished between two types of better-off peasants. One was the traditional kulak of pre-Revolutionary Russia, who hired workers, lent money and traded. The other was the successful small-scale farmer of more recent years. Smirnov believed that the first type no longer really existed. The revolution and subsequent land reforms and the Civil War had effectively wiped them out. The kulaks identified by Stalin were, for the most part, drawn from the second group. They were simply the most able peasants, the most efficient farmers and the group responsible for a large part of the Soviet Union's agricultural productivity.

Class war in the countryside

Stalin, however, refused to accept this. He believed that the NEP had allowed the traditional kulak to re-emerge. He was obsessed with the idea of this class of peasants opposing Soviet policy and hoarding grain. One attempt to define a kulak was to look at all the farmers who had between 25 and 40 sown acres. There were more than 1 million of these farmers (about 3.9% of the total peasantry, down from 15% before 1917). However, this was too small an amount for Stalin, so the Bolsheviks began to target a group that had expanded since the revolution. These were the *serednyaki*, or middle peasantry, who were essentially able and energetic farmers who farmed between 5 and 25 acres. They now accounted for some 60% of the total peasant population, but were hardly wealthy. It was this class that tended to get labelled as kulaks in the era of collectivisation, and many were shot, deported or sent to the gulag. But it was largely a phantom enemy. Stalin and his supporters approached the countryside wearing their Marxist spectacles and saw 'classes' and 'exploiters' instead of peasants. In doing so they created a 'class conflict' that needed to be resolved and decided there was an easy way to do it: with violence. In fact, as the historian Moshe Lewin stated, 'Who was the kulak? It is, in the first place, he who is declared to be such by the authorities.'

From the end of 1929 these various pressures conspired to create what was in effect a 'class war' in the countryside. Party activists identified kulaks on often slender evidence, while poorer peasants and rural workers were encouraged to attack their wealthier neighbours and seize their land and goods. Kulaks were publicly humiliated and forced into tar collars or beaten. Party leadership exploited divisions in rural communities with quotas for kulak arrests issued to local leaders. Civil disorder was also fomented in order to push through collectivisation. Small private plots and the independent market in agricultural products were destroyed in favour of large state-organised farms. Stalin was clear about the importance of this project. After announcing his Great Turn, he stated in November 1929 that 'either we succeed or we go under'. On 27 December 1929 Stalin raised the stakes still further, calling for the 'liquidation' of the 'kulaks as a class'.

The collective farms

But what would the new collective farms look like? How would they operate? On this the leadership was surprisingly vague. In fact it is doubtful whether they had a clear idea of what they were going to end up with. Stalin's vision of a collectivised Soviet Union was big on vision but small on detail. An All-Union Commissariat for Agriculture and a Commission for Collectivisation were set up to oversee the process but there is little evidence of their effectiveness. Instead it was left to local party leaders in alliance with party activists from the city, OGPU secret police units and the military to try to work out how to turn the theory into reality.

Generally the process went something like this. There was little guidance on the structure and organisation of the collective farms, so much of it was made up on the spot. A troika consisting of the local party committee secretary, the chairman of the regional or local soviet and the local OGPU chief carried out the process. They could rely on army units, party activists and OGPU forces to provide the muscle to back them up. Initially they would travel to a region and try to convince the local peasants to sign up to join a collective farm. For the most part, while the poorer peasants would do so, the wealthier would hesitate. These wealthier peasants would then be identified as kulaks and arrested, then either deported or shot. Their buildings and goods would be divided up and used in the new collective farms. Alongside the violence and anarchy of the anti-kulak operations the party attacked the Orthodox Church. Many priests were arrested and churches destroyed. Monasteries and convents were emptied and their inhabitants deported. A way of life that had lasted for centuries was destroyed, and many traditional peasant villages were effectively wiped out, incorporated into the new collective farms or abandoned.

Textbooks define three types of collective farm. First there was the *toz*. In this type of collective farm the peasants owned their own land but shared machinery and cooperated in activities such as sowing and harvesting. The second was the *sovkhoz*. This type of collective farm was owned and run by the state. The peasants who worked on this type of farm were paid a wage, rather like factory workers. The third type of collective farm was the *kolkhoz*. Here all the land was held in common and run by an elected committee. The collective farm comprised between 50 and 100 households. All land, livestock and tools were pooled and the peasants farmed the land as one unit. Each household was allowed to keep a small private plot of land of up to 1 acre. The leadership had hoped that the *sovkhoz* would be the main type of farm but peasant resistance effectively forced them to accept the *kolkhoz* as the main type.

In addition to this a network of MTS (machine and tractor stations) was planned. More than 2,500 of these were set up, and their purpose was to support the collective farms by providing machinery. They were also responsible for collecting grain quotas and were usually where the local party chief was based. In theory the peasants on the *kolkhoz* would be credited with workdays in exchange for their labour, and at the end of the year if the farm made any profits the workforce would share them. In reality little money was ever made, as the state requisitioned most of the produce, and in the first few years of collectivisation the chaos and disruption it caused meant that agricultural productivity plummeted. The peasants ended up forced to survive on the produce of their tiny plots and the few animals they were allowed to keep on them.

Most textbooks on the Soviet Union contain a pictorial representation of what a 'typical' or 'ideal' collective farm looked like. Such diagrams normally give an impression of planning and orderliness, with the MTS connected to the collective farm, various communal buildings and processing plants scattered about, and some private plots looking rather homely and well-tended, with little stick-men driving tractors and tending the fields. This might have been what collective farms ended up looking like decades later, but few would have looked like this in 1930–32, when the process was taking place. In fact most collective farms were chaotic and improvised affairs. A look at the statistics will give us a clearer idea of why this was.

There were more than 120 million peasants living in the countryside at this time who would be affected by these changes. They lived in some 600,000 villages. The state planned to consolidate the 25 million peasant holdings into some 240,000 collective farms under state control. This was to be achieved in a matter of 2 or 3 years at most. In fact Stalin announced in the summer of 1929 that 7.8 million peasant holdings were to be collectivised by the end of 1930 (almost a third). At the same time as the peasants were collectivised, the kulaks were initially isolated and then 'liquidated' (either shot, deported or sent to the gulag). Estimates vary as to how many kulaks were dealt with in this way, but the most likely figure is about 10 million. These were often the most able and successful farmers and their loss was not easily made up. Stalin remained unconcerned, and on 27 December 1929 he told a group of Marxist students, 'To take the offensive against the kulaks means to deal the kulak class such a blow that it will no longer rise to its feet. That's what we Bolsheviks call an offensive.'

Questions

1 Why was collectivisation carried out so rapidly?

2 How was collectivisation carried out?

3 To what extent was collectivisation a 'socialist' solution to the problems of the NEP?

What were the consequences of collectivisation?

Collectivisation was essentially a militaristic operation by the state against the peasantry. An illusion of populist support was created by the regime through a propaganda campaign, but in reality Stalin wanted to move the peasantry into collective farms so that he could procure more grain and destroy their independence, and because he felt it was a more 'socialist' or 'Marxist' solution. There was also the matter of the long-running hostility between the party and the peasants. Menzhinsky (head of the OGPU at this stage) had declared, 'The peasants are cattle to be sacrificed to the revolution.' Stalin too had talked of peasants as 'cattle' and of Lenin as the 'cattle drover'. The whole process of collectivisation was supported by an army of activists and on occasion military units, but chiefly by the OGPU. Menzhinsky had stated in his doctoral thesis in 1898 that the 'peasant commune...is one of the major brakes on Russia's agricultural development...the commune is disintegrating, dying a natural death'. It is therefore no surprise that he was to be such an enthusiastic supporter of Stalin's attempts to finally kill it off.

Opposition

In mid-1929 fewer than 5% of the country's peasants were in collective farms. In January 1930 Stalin announced that around 25% of the grain-producing areas were to be collectivised by the end of the year. On 5 January Stalin and the Central Committee doubled and even trebled the initial targets. This announcement took even his own party by surprise, as they had assumed the process would be voluntary and gradual. In a *Pravda* article on 7 November 1929 entitled 'Year of the Great Breakthrough' Stalin had stated, 'Peasants are joining the collective farms not in separate groups, but in whole villages, whole regions, whole districts and even whole provinces.' This was certainly untrue, but he wanted to convince the party that collectivisation was the key to the future success of the USSR. He stated, 'We are advancing full steam ahead along the path to industrialisation — to Socialism, leaving behind the age-long "Russian" backwardness. We are becoming a country of metal, a country of automobiles, a country of tractors.'

The January announcements and decrees were the national signal for collectivisation to be pushed through in earnest. Vyacheslav Molotov (a leading member of the Politburo) called for decisive action over the next few months. Stalin was calling for the completion of collectivisation in the Ukraine, the North Caucasus and the Middle Volga (the USSR's chief grain-producing areas) within 1 or 2 years. The state redoubled its efforts to stir up hatred of the kulak class in the countryside with a wave of arrests and denunciations (a strategy it was finding difficult to implement, with most villages resisting the pressure to identify 'enemies within'). Some 25,000 party activists from cities were sent out to lend support to OGPU units. A further 72,000 workers were added to these groups in the spring of 1930 and more than 50,000 soldiers also joined the campaign.

The large numbers of troops deployed in the collectivisation operations were testimony to the growing resistance to the policy. It is not surprising that many peasants opposed the whole process. They were being asked to abandon farms owned for generations in exchange for a very uncertain future. It was not as if the new collective farms were prepared and waiting for families to move in. They usually did not even exist when farmers were being asked to sign up for them, and the process by which they were created was chaotic and unplanned. Issues such as what land you received, where you relocated to and how you were supplied and paid were all something of a lottery in 1929 and 1930. Nevertheless the process continued. On 1 March 1930 Stalin announced that since January the number of collectivised households had risen from 4,393,100 to 14,264,300 (a total of 59%). As the pressure on the peasants to collectivise mounted, resistance flared.

In 1930–31 there were more than 2,200 rebellions in the countryside, involving some 800,000 people. Armoured trains were sent into the provinces along with OGPU units and battalions of soldiers. Anastas Mikoyan, one of Stalin's trusted party bosses, who had been sent out to Siberia to deal with rebellions, wrote, 'We face big resistance...we need to destroy the resistance.' Alongside open rebellion, peasants were reacting by slaughtering their animals rather than hand them over to the state. They had killed 14 million out of the country's 1928 total of 70.5 million cattle, a third of all pigs and a quarter of all sheep and goats. Mikhail Sholokhov described this in his novel *Virgin Soil Upturned* (1935):

> Kill, it's not ours any more…Kill, they'll take it for meat anyway…Kill, you won't get meat on the collective farm…And they killed. They ate until they could eat no more. Young and old suffered from stomach ache…At dinnertime tables groaned under boiled and roasted meat. At dinner time everyone had a greasy mouth…everyone blinked like an owl, as if drunk from eating.

On 16 January 1930 the party decreed that kulaks' property could be seized if they destroyed their livestock. Even Stalin was worried by reports of such wholesale slaughter and he decided on a strategic pause. In a speech reported in *Pravda* on 2 March 1930 under the title 'Dizzy with Success' Stalin carried out an extraordinary public volte-face. He reproved party activists for their actions and stated, 'Collective farms cannot be set up by force. To do so would be stupid and reactionary. The collective farm movement must rely on the active support of the great bulk of the peasantry.' This speech signalled a temporary pause in the process, one in which more than 9 million families left the collectives. By October 1930 the 1 March figure of 59% of households collectivised had fallen to 22% and it seemed Stalin had compromised in the face of overwhelming opposition. In an attempt to encourage peasants to stay, those in *kolkhoz* farms were allowed to keep a cow, sheep and pigs and a private plot of their own. Those leaving faced difficulty in securing land, tools and seeds and were given harsher quotas. Many were arrested in succeeding waves of deportations and branded as kulaks by the authorities.

Despite the mass departures from the collective farms and the slaughter of livestock the collectivisation process was soon intensified. At the Sixteenth Party Congress in the summer of 1930 Stalin had stated that collectivisation was going to be a success and that the kulaks would be liquidated as a class. He said that the 'changeover to collective farms is the second and the decisive step which marks a most important stage in building the foundation of a socialist society in the USSR'. That year's harvest was the best since 1913 and seemed to confirm Stalin in his belief that his policy was the right course for the Soviet Union. Once the harvest was in, Stalin once more stepped up the pressure on the peasants, who again responded with a distinct lack of enthusiasm. Many fled to urban areas (more than 17.7 million between 1929 and 1935) and helped fuel the industrial expansion in the new cities. The government tried to stem this flow in 1932 by reintroducing internal passports (not seen since tsarist times), thereby tying the peasants to the land and the workers to their factories.

Those who stayed tried to survive as best they could. By the end of 1934 more than 70% of peasant households were collectivised, and this figure had risen to

90% by 1936. Peasant resistance had been broken. It had not been easy, however. The secretary of the Ukrainian Central Committee admitted this, stating:

> A ruthless struggle is going on between the peasantry and our regime. It is a struggle to the death. This year was a test of our strength and their endurance. It took a famine to show them who is master here. It has cost millions of lives, but the collective farms system is here to stay. We've won the war.

The most violent operations had been directed at the kulaks, and millions had been deported or shot. Abdurakhman Avtorkhanov wrote of the scene that greeted him at a railway station where he halted on his way to Moscow from Grozny in 1930. He had seen 'endless fields of people — women, children, old people — and universal wailing. They were being loaded on to cattle trucks to be sent off to Siberia. I was there for 15 minutes and I asked the stationmaster there, "What's this? What's happening here?" and he said, "What's up with you? Have you just landed from the moon, or maybe you've just arrived from Persia? This is collectivisation and the elimination of the kulaks as a class."'

The party leadership divided kulaks into three categories. The first category were deemed 'hostile' and were to be put into camps or shot. The second category were classified as 'dangerous' and were exiled to non-arable land in the north or in Kazakhstan. The third were classed as 'not posing a threat' and were simply dispossessed and left in their own region. By the end of 1930 Molotov's commission had put 210,000 households (2.5 million human beings) into the first two categories. Kulaks were evicted into the wilderness, with their neighbours forbidden to give them food or shelter. Their money and property were confiscated and those deported arrived to find neither housing nor any kind of infrastructure to support them.

A decree on 1 February 1930 had given local party organisations the power to use 'necessary measures' against the kulaks. This had led to whole families and even villages being rounded up and deported. In other instances they were simply shot. Others were sent to the gulag work camps or put into punishment brigades and sent off to build canals, railways, and the Metro in Moscow. V. Kravchenko, a Communist at the time, remembered the terrible chaos of the anti-kulak operations. He wrote of his experience of witnessing one such action:

> A large crowd was gathered outside the building…a number of women were weeping hysterically and calling the names of husbands and fathers. It was like a scene out of a nightmare…in the background, guarded by OGPU soldiers with drawn revolvers, stood about twenty peasants, young and old, with bundles on their backs. A few were weeping. The others stood there sullen, resigned, and hopeless. So this was the 'liquidation of the kulaks as a class!' A lot of simple peasants being torn from their native soil, stripped of their worldly goods and shipped off to some distant labour camps.

V. Serge, another party activist at the time, wrote:

> Trainloads of deported peasants left for the icy north, the forests, the steppes, the deserts. These were whole populations, denuded of everything; the old folk starved to death in mid-journey, newborn babies were buried on the banks of the roadside, and each wilderness had its little crop of crosses.

Hatred and hysteria whipped up by local party bosses also accounted for many deaths. Anti-kulak actions were encouraged; public humiliation and protests were orchestrated by the authorities. Informing was also encouraged, with one particularly infamous case of a 13-year-old girl being rewarded for telling the authorities her father was hoarding grain. In *Virgin Soil Unturned*, one of Sholokhov's characters (a party activist) makes the following statement about the kulaks: 'You could line up thousands of old men, women and children, and tell them they'd got to be crushed into dust for the sake of the revolution, and I'd shoot them all down with a machine gun.' This ruthless attitude, combined with a fervent belief in creating a Marxist state, allowed the party activists and military units involved in the anti-kulak operations to convince themselves that what they were doing was justifiable.

Lev Kopelev, an activist who later went into exile, stated:

> With the rest of my generation, I firmly believed that the ends justified the means. Our great goal was the universal triumph of communism…I saw what 'total collectivisation' meant — how they mercilessly stripped the peasants in the winter of 1932–33. I took part in it myself, scouring the countryside…testing the earth with an iron rod for loose spots that might lead to buried grain…I was convinced I was accomplishing the great and necessary transformation of the countryside; that in the days to come the people who lived there would be better off.

This belief allowed party members to close their eyes to the terrible suffering their policies caused. Once the kulaks had been deported, many died in remote areas of the Soviet Union. A survivor remembered that when they arrived in Kazakhstan, 'there were just some pegs stuck in the ground with little notices saying: Settlement No.5, No.6 and so on. The peasants were brought here and told that now they had to look after themselves. So there they dug themselves holes in the ground. A great many died of cold and hunger in the early years.'

In fact the attempt to colonise Kazakhstan with these kulak exiles was a complete disaster, as they arrived with no money, tools or grain stock and were simply left to wander around. The deported kulaks and the Soviet government also forced the Kazakhs to flee their native lands: up to 2 million of them, it is believed, into nearby China, where other Kazakh communities lived; up to half of these emigrants died.

The trains deporting the kulaks passed through urban areas: lines of cattle trucks carrying up to 2,000 deportees passed at walking pace through provincial cities. Local railway stations were overrun by these hordes of dispossessed peasants waiting to be shipped east. Tales of atrocities and large numbers of deaths on the long journeys into exile circulated, and even ardent party activists complained to regional authorities about the terrible fate of those deemed 'kulaks' or 'sub-kulaks'. There is no doubt that Stalin knew in detail about the fate of those he had decided were the obstacle to collectivisation. Genrikh Yagoda, Menzhinsky's right-hand man and later head of the NKVD, who was the senior OGPU official in charge of anti-kulak operations, sent detailed reports to Stalin and Molotov about the anti-kulak operations and the collectivisation campaigns. Furthermore, open warfare threatened across the Soviet Union as ethnic groups resisted Bolshevik actions, and chaos spread. Many communities were destroyed. In the south, Don Cossacks were murdered as 'kulaks' by Ukrainians, and other ethnic groups such as Chechens were executed as 'bandits'. The Volga Germans and Tatars resisted attempts to split kulaks from their communities, and OGPU units were called in to make sure that resistance was crushed. In 1929, some 35,000 Buryat Mongols were shot during 'pacification' of the region.

There are no exact figures for those killed in the anti-kulak operations, and it is difficult to arrive at a reliable estimate. By some reports, up to 10 million peasants or kulaks are believed to have been killed, deported or sent to labour camps. Robert Conquest puts the figure of total peasant deaths at 7.8 million (including the 1932–33 famine in the Ukraine and other areas), while others believe that it was lower. Donald Rayfield writes:

> Allowing for famine, violence, hypothermia and epidemics caused by the disruption, the number of excess deaths between 1930 and 1933 attributable to collectivisation lies between a conservative 7.2 and a plausible 10.8 million.

Many of these died of famine (an 'Auschwitz without ovens', as one survivor from the Ukraine put it). This famine was an inevitable consequence of Stalin's collectivisation policy. It was the final terrible phase of a process marked by violence and chaos throughout. The slaughter of livestock had devastated the Soviet Union's agricultural productivity, the round-up and deportation or execution of millions of kulaks had further eroded agricultural efficiency, and the chaotic transition to collective farms meant that farming in the USSR went into freefall. A further stress was the wholesale requisitioning of grain that continued throughout this period. It was often counter-productive, with activists stealing the supplies earmarked for sowing next year's fields. The situation was further exacerbated by Stalin's insistence that the peasants were hoarding grain, even when they weren't. By the end of 1931 the state had collected 22.8 million tons of grain, which was enough both to feed the cities and to send some for export. The capital raised by selling the grain was used to finance industrialisation and the Five-Year Plans.

Famine

But the worst was still to come. From 1930 to 1932 there was a wave of state-sponsored violence, including local incidents of massacre and 'liquidation' of resistance. OGPU units and the army were kept busy (in 1931 Yagoda recorded 20,000 acts of 'terrorist violence' in opposing collectivisation). The area that suffered the most in this period was the Ukraine. It became the focal point for Stalin's requisitioning policies, as he believed it should produce the most grain. He was also suspicious of Ukrainian nationalism and believed that the Ukraine harboured anti-Soviet forces. Stalin was convinced that the Ukraine needed special attention and that it was trying to resist the collectivisation drive. He accordingly increased targets, focusing his rage on those elements he believed were opposing his plans. Of all the kulaks deported, a quarter were Ukrainian.

In 1930 the Ukraine had accounted for 27% of the grain harvest but had been expected to supply 38% of the quota (a total of 7.7 million tons). In 1931, when there was a poorer harvest, the same quota of 7.7 million tons was demanded (even though only 18.3 million tons had been collected overall — down from 23.9 million). This meant the region had to give 42% of its total production over to the state. Seven million tons were collected, and by the spring of 1932 famine was already threatening the region; a drought made matters worse. In 1932 the total harvest came to 14.7 million tons, but the same quota was demanded. When the local party protested that such a quota was too much, its protests were ignored. The target was reduced to 6.6 million tons but the Ukrainian Central Committee still failed to meet it. Stalin increased the pressure on the local party: on 7 August 1932 a new decree made it a capital offence to steal collective farm property, and even stealing small amounts of grain could result in sentences of up to 10 years. The peasants called this the 'five-stalks' law (from the small amount of grain needed to be sentenced) or the 'law of seven-eighths' (as it was passed on the seventh day of the eighth month). By the end of 1932, more than 55,000 people had been sentenced for violating it, and in the Kharkov region more than 1,500 were killed.

By the end of 1932 only 4.7 million tons of grain had been collected and famine was rife. When Terekhov, the first secretary of Kharkov, protested to Stalin about the famine, he was told that he was a 'good story teller…why don't you leave your post as regional secretary and the Central Committee and go to work for the Writers' Union? You could write fables and folk could read them.' A third attempt to meet the target was ordered; local officials were replaced and new activists drafted in. By March 1933 the farming system in the region had effectively collapsed under the strain of repeated procurements and millions began to die. The reserves of grain collected by Stalin for export remained in storage and the starving inhabitants of the Ukraine were left to fend for themselves. The USSR exported 1.73 million tons of grain in 1932 and only slightly less in 1933. In some instances warehouses of grain were left to rot while people in nearby towns and cities starved to death. Again, as in the anti-kulak operations, exact figures for the dead are hard to come by. Khrushchev summed this up when he stated, 'No one was keeping count…all we knew was that people were dying in enormous numbers.'

The famine that swept the Ukraine in 1932–33 was not widely reported within or outside the Soviet Union. There are few photos or surviving accounts of the terrible suffering of the people in the hardest-hit areas. What is clear, though, is that this was a man-made famine, and while it may not have been explicit policy to starve the region and force it into submission, this was clearly a useful by-product of the disaster as far as the party leadership was concerned. What accounts there are of the famine are horrific. Alisa Maslo remembers the events that occurred in the village of Targan, where 362 people died in the famine:

> They went from house to house and they took away everything to the last grain…and this included ours. And they really left the family to certain famine death. And so my grandma dies and then one of my brothers…my mother was lying in bed swollen with hunger…my other brother died. And I told my mother that 'we're the only two left', that my brother was also dead. Up came the cart and the man took my brother and dragged him to the cart, and then my own *live* mother. I started crying and the man said, 'Go to the orphanage where at least you'll get some soup. She will die anyway, why should I come here a second time?' And so I became an orphan.

Alexandra Ovdiuk, a school student at the time, remembers that 'in 1933 it really was frightening. Every day someone did not show up for school. The children were very scared and all swollen up. I'll never forget this. There were a lot of them that died in our class.' There were even accounts of cannibalism caused by the terrible hunger. A neighbour of Mykola Pishy resorted to this:

> Ivan was a good specialist — a joiner, a tailor, a shoe-maker — a good fellow who could turn his hand to anything. But the famine was awful and he got to the end of his tether. He was so hungry that he killed his child and ate the meat — of his own child. His wife was dead scared. She went to the village council to report on him. She told how her husband had gone mad and had killed his own child. So he was taken away. No one knows where.

Despite the awfulness of conditions in the Ukraine, party activists continued to seize grain. Lev Kopelev recalls that they did not discuss the famine, 'because we were convinced that the disaster was not so much the fault of the Party and State, as a result of inexorable "objective" circumstances. We were convinced the famine was caused by the opposition of suicidally unconscientious peasants, enemy intrigues and the inexperience and weakness of the lower ranks of workers.'

Officials higher in the party refused to accept that there was a famine and party activists became wary of reporting it. One activist who did was the husband of Sara Babyonysheva. He was in charge of requisition squads in the north Caucasus and reported to the Regional Party Committee in a telegram that 'there is no wheat, people were dying of starvation, help them'. He was expelled from the party and later arrested; he died in a labour camp. While the peasants were eating 'dogs, horses, rotten potatoes, the bark of trees, anything they could find' (Fyodor Belov), Stalin remained in his country house or working in Moscow. It was obvious that collectivisation was causing terrible suffering but Stalin refused to accept criticism or admit the famine was happening. On 18 June 1932 Stalin talked of the 'glaring absurdities' of reports of famine in the Ukraine and refused to give any credence to accounts of it. His wife Nadezhda was less easily persuaded and there is some evidence that growing disquiet about the reports of starvation reaching her at work caused tension in her marriage to Stalin. In November 1932 she shot herself. Whatever the reason for her suicide, it served to heighten Stalin's sense of desperation and alienation and began to ratchet up tension prior to the purges that ensued.

The year that followed, 1933, was probably the most critical one as far as Stalin was concerned. The whole success of collectivisation hung in the balance. Farming productivity had plunged, millions were dying and party authority in the countryside was collapsing. One of the few Western visitors to witness the terrible scale of the suffering in the Soviet countryside was British journalist Malcolm Muggeridge, who travelled to the Ukraine from Moscow. He wrote, 'The fields are neglected and full of weeds, no cattle are to be seen anywhere and few horses, only the military and OGPU are well fed, the rest of the population obviously starving, obviously terrorised.' Stalin fretted in Moscow. He wrote to Kosior, a member of the Politburo and Ukrainian party leader, 'It seems that in some regions of the Ukraine, Soviet power has ceased to exist. Is this true? Is the situation so bad in Ukrainian villages? What's the GPU doing? Maybe you'll check this problem and take measures.' These 'measures' would inevitably be more armed requisition squads, more arrests and more terror. At this stage Stalin was relying on his most loyal and ruthless party chiefs to sort out the problems collectivisation was throwing up. Worried by reports of dissent in the Caucasus, he sent Lavrenti Beria (later head of the NKVD and one of Stalin's toughest lieutenants) out to the region. Beria become Georgian First Secretary and Second Secretary of Transcaucasia and soon ensured that the region was brought to heel.

Another of Stalin's allies during the period was Lazar Kaganovich, known by the nickname 'Iron Lazar'. He was typical of the new breed of Stalinists that now ruled the party. Promoted through the ranks of the party by Lenin, he had demonstrated sufficient ruthlessness in the Civil War to be noticed by party chiefs. He had run Central Asia for the party in 1924, and in 1925 was put in charge of the Ukraine. He was made a member of the Politburo in 1930. In this time of crisis Stalin sent him back to the Ukraine to make sure the republic stayed within the party's control. Stalin, despite public denials that any such event was occurring, was secretly worried about the effects of the famine and wrote to Kaganovich, 'If we don't make an effort now to improve the situation in the Ukraine, we may lose the Ukraine.' Once Kaganovich had 'improved' the Ukraine he was sent to the Kuban region to quash dissent. Mass reprisals against the Cossacks followed, along with the deportation of 15 villages.

It seems that Stalin and his party leaders revelled in such actions. Simon Sebag Montefiore writes of the Communist Party 'magnates' who were:

> hardened by years in the underground, blood-splattered by their exploits in the Civil War, and now exultant if battered by the industrial triumphs and rural struggles of the Stalin revolution…some of the most dynamic administrators the world has ever seen, capable of building towns and factories against all odds, but also of slaughtering their enemies and waging war on their own peasants. In their tunics and boots they were macho, hard-drinking, powerful and famous across the Imperium, stars with blazing egos, colossal responsibilities, and Mausers in their holsters.

These were the men who bent Soviet Russia to their will and pushed through collectivisation, whatever the cost. This was why, despite his fears, throughout the period Stalin remained unmoved by any pleas for mercy, accounts of starvation or appeals to ease the pressure. He told Winston Churchill in 1943 that it had been the most difficult time of his life. He stated that it was 'a terrible struggle' in which he had had to destroy '…ten million. It was fearful. Four years it lasted. It was absolutely necessary…it was no use arguing with them. A certain number had to be resettled in the northern parts of the country…others had been slaughtered by the peasants themselves — such had been the hatred of them.'

Despite the starvation, the mass arrests, the riots and the violence, by 1934 the main work of collectivisation had been achieved. The 'kulaks' (whoever they were) had been destroyed and opposition eliminated or silenced. The Ukraine and other regions had been essentially starved into submission. Stalin had weathered the crisis and remained party leader. By 1936, 90% of peasant households had been collectivised, but how successful was the policy of collectivisation? Did it improve agricultural efficiency? Was the socialist solution to farming the correct one? Collectivisation in the short term was disastrous. The slaughter of livestock dramatically reduced meat production and the famine led to the most productive areas of the Soviet Union becoming the most impoverished. Added to this was the human cost. Millions died of starvation; millions more were deported or executed.

Donald Rayfield writes that the:

> suffering that ensued has few parallels in human history; it can only be compared in its scale and monstrosity with the African slave trade. But whereas the British, French, Spanish and Portuguese took 200 years to transport some 10 million souls into slavery, and kill about 2 million of them, Stalin matched this figure in a matter of 4 years. This was an act of unprecedented monstrosity, and the almost total silence and indifference of Europe and the USA to the fate of the Russian peasantry suggests that the rest of the world, like Lenin, Stalin and Menzhinsky, considered the Russian peasant hardly human. This then is an undeniable aspect of the operation. It was in many ways a holocaust unleashed on the countryside of Russia by a terroristic state and this alone should be enough to condemn it.

Collectivisation ensured the destruction of the most able peasant farmers and the end of a traditional way of life in rural Russia that had endured for centuries. The persecution of the church, the closing of monasteries and the exile of thousands of priests, nuns and monks were further consequences of Stalin's great project. The peasants referred to collectivisation as a 'second serfdom'. They were tied to land they did not own. They could not leave their farms without the permission of the authorities and they faced harsh punishments if they tried to act independently. In many ways their situation was worse than it had been before their 1861 emancipation by Alexander II. Grain production recovered slowly but did not exceed pre-collectivisation levels until 1935. Meat production did not pass pre-collectivisation levels until after Stalin's death in 1953.

Collectivisation also destroyed any incentive to make up this shortfall. The peasants were supposed to get a share of the profits of the collective farm but there were rarely any profits to share. They focused instead on their own private plots of land. They could sell any excess produce they farmed here to local markets. These private plots were far more productive than the collective farms. It has been estimated that in post-collectivisation USSR these private plots produced 52% of vegetables, 57% of fruit, 70% of meat and 71% of butter, honey and wool. The state so desperately needed this produce that the authorities effectively turned a blind eye to the situation. Collectivisation was the public face of Soviet farming; in private it relied on local private enterprise. In addition to this the peasants were imaginative in their ploys to evade communal obligations and often did little real work on the collective farms.

Subjugation

An illuminating case study of the collectivisation process and its consequences has been preserved in the Smolensk archive. The US authorities seized these records from Berlin in 1945. They had been captured by the Germans after retreating Soviet forces abandoned the city of Smolensk in 1941. For many years they represented one of the few glimpses Western historians had of the working of the Soviet regime in its own words. They contain considerable detail on the collectivisation in the region. Before collectivisation, 90% of the population in the Smolensk region were farmers. In 1927, 5% of these farmers were classed as kulaks, 70% as middle peasants and 25% as poor peasants. From 1928 those in the kulak class were targeted by the authorities and forced to pay fines, heavy taxes, and high wages for labourers. After 1928 this perse-cution became more overt and activists were sent to the region to enlist the help of the middle peasants against the kulaks. They found that local people were reluctant to support this campaign and the regional soviets and party leaders were siding with the peasants.

Party activists therefore stepped up the pressure on the peasant communities. They were given fixed quotas, and if they failed to produce them grain was seized and they were often punished. The peasants resisted: in October 1929 ten chairmen and eight party secretaries were murdered. The OGPU was called in and more terroristic methods used to subdue the villages. Court cases show that half of those tried were poor or middle peasants and they were branded ideological kulaks. Then the first big collectivisation drive hit Smolensk and the violence radically shifted upwards. 'Shock' brigades of military units and activists descended on the villages. Panic spread as kulaks sold off all their possessions and abandoned their farms. Many fled to the cities or to the Urals and there was a wave of suicides as peasant households killed themselves rather than face deportation. Solidarity among the villagers survived the attempts to undermine communal bonds and there were shows of support for the kulaks from their poorer neighbours.

Farmers did not like the *kolkhoz* system. Thousands of letters of protest were sent to local papers. In September 1929, 200 peasants attacked one *kolkhoz*. Many women joined in such attacks and protests, and the OGPU was forced to arrest whole villages and families. A second wave of repression followed in March 1931, with more kulaks arrested, and the drive to collectivise continued. Like the rest of the country, Smolensk was eventually collectivised and by the end of the 1930s relative calm had been restored. Nevertheless, the whole region had been traumatised by the events of 1929–33. Collective bonds had been broken, communities destroyed and thousands of locals killed or deported.

A region that experienced particularly severe suffering during the collectivisation process was the Mongolian People's Republic. Although nominally an independent country, this was effectively part of the USSR. The Buddhist lamas (a third of the adult male population of Mongolia) were executed and the cattle herders dispossessed. By spring 1932 the total population of the country had been reduced by a third. The result was widespread rebellion and some relaxation of the terror by the authorities.

How successful was collectivisation?

In terms of economic productivity the result of collectivisation was negative. Figures for the grain harvest show a dramatic dip: in 1928, 73.3 million tons were produced, but by 1932 total production had fallen to 69.6 million tons, and it did not recover until 1935. Cattle production fell from 70.5 million animals in 1928 to 40.1 million in 1932. If we look at the figures for sheep we can see that there were 146.7 million of them in 1928, and by 1932 this had fallen to 52.1 million. By 1935 the total had risen slightly to 61.1 million (still less than half of pre-collectivisation levels).

Stalin's motivations for collectivisation were complex, however, and economics was only one factor. Stalin had two other principal aims when he collectivised. He wanted to control the peasantry and bring them into the Communist state, and he also wanted to increase the state's ability to procure grain. He wanted grain to sell abroad so that he could raise money for industrialisation, but he also wanted to secure grain supplies for the urban workers. If we take into account these motivations it is easier to argue that collectivisation was successful in some senses, in that it achieved what Stalin wanted.

In 1928–29 the state collected 10.8 million tons of grain. By 1931–32 it had managed to increase this to 22.8 million tons. This represented a significant shift in its ability to secure food for the cities and for export abroad. After collectivisation the state could guarantee it could feed the cities, crucial to the success of the party's modernisation and development drives. Perhaps the most important cause (and consequence) of collectivisation was that Stalin had broken the peasantry and forced them to accept the new Bolshevik order. The ancient way of life of the village *mir*, with its almost autonomous place in the Russian order of things, was no more. It had been destroyed, the peasants either collectivised, deported or dead. Resistance had been crushed without mercy, and Stalin had succeeded in securing grain for industrialisation and export. The Soviet writer Lyudmila Saraskina summarised this well when she wrote:

> If you imagine that Stalin wanted to improve the harvest or to improve the lot of the peasant, then you're just fooling yourself…Collectivisation was a bloody, terrible and monstrous means of the seizure of absolute power because the free peasant and the master of the land, the farmer, constituted one of the main obstacles on the path to the absolute feudal power that Stalin wanted.

Some historians have argued that collectivisation should be put into context alongside other European states' experience of modernisation, and have noted that in such a contest the peasantry lose out to modernising influences. They point out that at some stage the conflict between a modernising state and a backward peasantry would have had to occur. The Bolsheviks wanted the Soviet Union to join the ranks of the advanced industrial nations to the west (Britain, France, Germany and Belgium) and to the east (Japan). The peasants had proved that they would not necessarily cooperate in the transformation of the country into a modern urban society. In the so-called 'Scissors Crisis' of 1923 the peasants had reacted to rising retail prices for manufactured goods by sowing less and threatening to retreat into subsistence farming; the party had been forced to reduce retail prices. In 1926–28 a looming grain procurement crisis had also caused alarm and convinced party leaders that some kind of reckoning was inevitable. As Chris Ward writes:

> Stalin stumbled into a bloody civil war with the peasants, but he stumbled along a path which the Party, increasingly reflecting his own ideological proclivities, was already inclined to take. In this sense and in this sense alone, collectivisation — or something very like it — was, as Stalinist historians believed, Russia's destiny.

However, while Ward might state that 'for two centuries modernisation has entailed the death agony of the peasantry and of traditional societies everywhere', the wholesale slaughter of collectivisation should be viewed in a very different category. Donald Rayfield states that 'Stalin's campaign of 1929 against the peasantry might be seen by a cold-blooded cynic as a long overdue cure for an overpopulated countryside', but you would have to be a very cold-blooded cynic indeed to concur.

What is amazing is how little comment collectivisation aroused abroad. The massive and chaotic spasm that transformed the rural Soviet Union and destroyed a whole class of peasants was rarely reported. Western commentators such as the British professor Bernard Pares or the *New York Times* journalist

Walter Duranty stated that nothing exceptional was occurring. Information about it was strictly controlled, and the vastness of the Soviet Union, combined with the naturally secretive nature of the Communist regime, meant that while some news of it filtered out, the process was not really grasped in its monstrous entirety. British socialists such as George Bernard Shaw and Beatrice and Sidney Webb visited the country at the height of the famine and arrests yet saw nothing, even reporting back that the 'socialist utopia' was being created. Alexander Solzhenitsyn was more perceptive and wrote of this 'non-recurring tidal wave' (of dispossessed kulaks) that 'swelled beyond the bounds of anything the penal system of even an immense state can permit itself. There was nothing to be compared with it in all Russian history. It was the forced resettlement of a whole people, an ethnic catastrophe.'

Collectivisation was thus (for Stalin) a necessary prerequisite of modernisation. The peasants were part of 'old Russia', the Russia that had been defeated again and again by its more advanced neighbours. Stalin and the Bolshevik leadership believed that the nation needed to modernise, and if that involved the breaking of a whole class of people, that was the price that had to be paid. The important objective was that Stalin should remain unopposed and able to industrialise rapidly. The process also gave Stalin complete control over the Soviet Union, as Rayfield writes:

Collectivisation had brutalised victims and perpetrators to such a degree that civilised society no longer existed in the USSR. The cruelty and passivity it induced in Soviet citizens made it possible for Stalin and his hangmen to proceed to an even more violent campaign in the Party and among the urban population.

Was there another path? Historians have puzzled about this question. The fact that Stalin won the Second World War has in some sense been presented as a vindication of his economic, industrial and social policies in the 1930s. There is some support for this, as the economic might of the Soviet Union and its ability to outproduce Germany was crucial in the success of the Soviet forces. However, it is difficult to argue that collectivisation was necessarily helpful in this, and in fact Stalin's terrible blunders in 1941 and his refusal to accept reports of German preparations could equally be seen as having brought the Soviet Union to the brink of defeat. Could the Soviet state have modernised effectively without such a terrible cost in human lives and economic chaos? The answer surely must be yes. Some historians have looked at Bukharin and his supporters and argued that their more moderate gradualist policies could have worked. Perhaps if Kirov (assassinated in 1934) had accepted the role of General Secretary when dissident elements in the party had offered it to him in 1933 and ousted Stalin, the Soviet Union could have avoided the worst excesses of the Terror (which in 1933 were still to come — although for the kulaks it was already too late). Looking at the raw economic data, it would be hard to argue that collectivisation was successful. However, much more was at stake than the purely economic, and when we consider the direction that the party leadership was taking in 1927–28, collectivisation becomes more understandable as a policy. Had the peasants been allowed to continue with the NEP for that intervening decade things might have been very different.

These questions are still very controversial. The current state of Russia, following the collapse of the USSR in 1991, has added extra importance to them. Some former Soviet states, such as Georgia, have effectively collapsed since the fall of communism, while the Russian Federation in general has been economically backward when compared with the West. More recently its economy has enjoyed a revival of fortunes thanks to energy production and its oil and gas reserves, but farming is still a weak sector of the economy and some would blame this on Stalin and collectivisation. However, collectivisation was only one of the two main strands that were to define the Soviet Union in the 1930s, and it was in a sense the platform for the policy of rapid industrialisation that Stalin embarked on in his 'Great Turn' in 1928–29. Collectivisation provided the capital for investment and food for the cities, and although it was not an intended effect, the process also provided much of the labour that made industrialisation possible, both in the camps and in the new cities springing up across the country. The cost of collectivisation in terms of the trauma suffered by the population forced to endure it cannot be calculated, and unlike postwar Germany, in Russia there has been no reckoning. As Lev Razgon (a one-time party member imprisoned at the height of the Terror in 1938) wrote:

> There were many more involved in these murders than those who simply pulled the trigger…today they are all retired and receive large individual pensions…they are alive and there are many of them…the murderers are among us. And there is nothing we can do about it.

Questions

1 What impact did collectivisation have on the peasants?
2 Was collectivisation a success?
3 What were the results of collectivisation in the 1930s?

How did Stalin industrialise the Soviet Union?

The failure of Russia to industrialise effectively had been one of the main stumbling blocks to its success in the nineteenth century. While in 1815 Russia had been a 'great power', able to take its place at the Congress of Vienna and to help carve up Europe after the fall of Napoleon, it rapidly fell behind the Western powers of Prussia, France and Britain. There were a number of reasons for this. First, Russia was huge and much of the country was uninhabitable. Vast tracts of land were tundra, frozen soil which could not be cultivated. Other great swathes of the country were forest, or under snow for large parts of the year. In 1900 the country made up one sixth of the world's landmass. It stretched 6,400 kilometres from west to east and 3,000 kilometres from north to south. Despite losing land to the new Polish state after 1918 it was still enormous. Second, communications were terrible. There was just one railway that crossed Russia, the trans-Siberian railway that started in Moscow and ended in Vladivostok. Roads were generally poor, and rivers rather than roads had traditionally served the cities.

Continuing a bloody tradition

Russia had a tradition of government-led development. Peter the Great had founded factories, mines and shipyards in the Urals, the Volga district and St Petersburg. Linking his capital to the sea had cost untold deaths, and it has been claimed that up to 50,000 workers died gilding St Isaac's Cathedral in St Petersburg. Catherine the Great had drawn up plans to harness the waters of the River Dnepr. In the 1840s the railway construction boom had been initiated by Nicholas I, while Alexander III had pressed for rapid industrialisation because of his increasing worry about war with the Western powers. In 1907 the duma had called for a 7-year plan to exploit Siberia, and even the NEP, for all its compromises, was essentially a state-managed economy. To some extent Stalin, in adopting the mantle of moderniser, was following an illustrious if bloody tradition. He admired autocratic tsars such as Ivan the Terrible and Peter the Great who had imposed their will on Russia and made it great. Simon Sebag Montefiore notes, 'He regarded Ivan the Terrible as his true *alter ego*, his "teacher", something he revealed constantly to comrades such as Molotov, Zhdanov and Mikoyan, applauding his necessary murder of over-mighty *boyars* (nobles)'. Stalin saw himself as a great Russian leader and believed that if he had to take murderous steps to achieve his goals, that was the price that had to be paid.

As an empire Russia also faced the complex issue of nationalities. Under the tsars the policy had been to 'Russianise' the empire. Everyone was expected to speak Russian, and all government communication and education was in Russian. Local nationalities had been repressed. Ethnic Russians made up only about half of the population and were mainly concentrated in the urbanised west, focused on the cities of Moscow and St Petersburg. It is important to remember that many Russians were from areas lying outside Russia proper, such as Turkmenistan and the Ukraine. The Bolsheviks had initially promised a large measure of independence to these areas, but the Civil War and Lenin's desire to centralise had soon led to this policy being reversed. There was more freedom for the localities in one sense, as local parties were allowed to use their own language and develop their own party elite, but essentially they were under the control of the Moscow-based party. This had been proved bloodily in the Civil War by leaders such as Stalin in Georgia and Kaganovich in the Ukraine, who repressed any hint of attempts at independence.

The communication problem, allied to the issue of such national and ethnic diversity, had slowed modernisation and made it difficult for the centre to impose policies across the nation. Russia was well behind the Western powers on a whole range of modernising indices. Its performance in terms of literacy, primary education, secondary schooling, policing, civil servants and university graduates was well below that of countries such as France and Britain. In addition to this, Russia suffered from having its raw materials located some distance from its urban areas. Its oil reserves were mainly in the south, around the Caucasus and the Black and Caspian Seas. Its ores were mainly in the east, and much of its gold, copper and uranium was in the inhospitable north and Siberia. Access to the sea was limited, with much of the coast cut off in winter by ice. There was also a shortage of raw materials such as coal, as mining was still in its infancy. These issues, combined with a predominantly peasant population and agrarian economy, were serious obstacles to modernisation.

Russia had experienced a rude awakening to its lagging development during the Crimean War of 1853–56. Taking on a coalition of the Ottoman empire,

Britain and France, it had found itself having to fight much harder than expected and did not emerge victorious. Alexander II used this defeat to push through emancipation of the serfs in 1861, which proved partly successful. The serfs were freed but remained tied to the land by large debts. Alexander had attempted to reform the army, reducing military service and trying to create a professional officer class. There had also been some attempts to industrialise. However, these 'reformers', as the men around Alexander II who had tried to push through modernisation were known, were in conflict with traditionalists who saw attempts to make economic changes and increase social mobility as dangerous, subversive and even 'un-Russian'. The main model for development at this stage was Britain. Liberals in Russia admired its social stability, representative government and economic success, but were unsure how to replicate it.

The assassination of Alexander II in March 1881 settled the argument in favour of the traditionalists. His son Alexander III was an 'old-school' autocrat who saw the new forces of liberalism and democracy as dangerous. Repression and censorship were widespread, and conservative political leaders such as Konstantin Pobedonostsev encouraged him to avoid change and remain wedded to the 'old' Russia. The sudden death of Alexander III in 1894 thrust the inexperienced and unprepared Nicholas II into the role of the tsar and left the fundamental arguments over the direction of Russia unresolved. Should Russia modernise like the West? This would involve embracing more democracy and liberalism, opening up education and generally encouraging freedom of trade, capital and ideas. Or should Russia maintain its isolation and relative backwardness, which would preserve tsarist power but leave the country open to more foreign humiliation if there was another great power conflict? Essentially, Nicholas vacillated. He allowed his economic minister Sergei Witte to push through limited modernisation and development. Witte funded industrial expansion by raising foreign loans and selling grain. He increased investment in railways and construction and began to create an urbanised workforce employed in factories. There was also a corresponding growth in educated graduates and specialists able to help plan economic development. But he avoided full-scale modernisation as this would open up dangerous cracks in the Russian autocracy, and by 1900 Russia was still a 'backward', semi-feudal society. An economic depression that started in 1902 brought Witte's plans to a halt and the economy struggled with bad harvests, high unemployment and slow growth.

In addition to this, Russia embarked on a war with Japan. It was largely a conflict over trading rights in Korea. Initially it was a diplomatic incident, but the Russians' certainty of beating their racial inferiors, the Japanese, pushed them into war. Their breathtaking arrogance and racist conviction that the

Japanese would be smashed was soon corrected, and the final humiliation of losing their entire fleet off Japan sparked revolution at home. The tsar narrowly survived the riots and mutinies of 1905 and was forced to concede rights to an elected body, the duma. But before long he was busy imprisoning and executing his domestic opponents. His chief minister, Stolypin, repressed dissent in the cities but tried to modernise the countryside. In 1905, emancipation debts had been wiped clean. Now he tried to create a class of prosperous peasants (kulaks). He had the idea that if he could establish this, effectively a rural middle class, he could create an internal market for manufactured goods and thereby kick-start an economic recovery. In this he was looking primarily at Prussia, where small rural landholders had helped finance the expansion of the factories. Such a move, if allied with massive investment and a serious attempt to modernise and educate the Russian workforce, could have worked had the tsar not embarked on another war. Stolypin prayed for '20 years of peace' in 1907 but he got less than a decade.

Overall, Russia had made some progress towards modernisation in the later tsarist period. By 1913 industrial output was more than ten times the level of 1860 and Russia's aggregate output made it the fifth largest producer in the world. However, this had largely been achieved by state intervention and there was little grass-roots capitalism. Industrialisation was achieved by foreign investment under state control, and much of the pre-1914 growth was connected with expansion of the armed forces. There was still only a small middle class and an even smaller entrepreneurial class, and much of the industrial capital remained in foreign investors' control. Heavy industry was large-scale and often organised by syndicates, while the consumer sector was weak and relied mainly on imports. What the tsarist state needed was time to allow for development to spread beyond the control of the state and a few foreign companies. Stability would be the key to success, yet the tsar's decision to mobilise his armed forces in defence of Serbian interests in 1914 doomed his system to collapse. Three hundred years of Romanov rule ended with the decision to go to war with Germany.

The relative backwardness of Russia's economic development was brought into terrible focus by its decision to take on Germany. It could just about hold its own against Austria-Hungary (another antiquated empire based largely on a feudal economy, wealthy nobles and small urban centres) but was totally outclassed by Germany. Germany was a predominantly literate, urban and advanced society with the best army in Europe. It took Britain, France and the USA almost 4 years to muster the resources to begin to defeat it. Russia did not stand a chance. Its huge conscript forces were slaughtered in their millions, and despite some limited successes in the 1916 Brusilov offensive the Russian army was effectively crushed. By 1917 the Russians were suing for peace, the tsar was forced into exile and the Provisional Government was in power. The liberal coalition that it was mustering was no match for the organised soviets and by October 1917 the Bolsheviks were in charge.

Once in power, the Bolsheviks became the Communist Party and took ownership of all heavy industry, the banking sector and railways, and they were keen to extinguish private enterprise altogether if they could. Here finally was a party that was very keen to modernise. In fact the whole raison d'être of the party was industrialisation. They were the party of the urban workers, the factories and the city. They were the disciples of Karl Marx who saw the future of the world built in concrete with the factory at its centre and an urban workforce as its main citizens. While for the tsars modernisation was an incon-venient necessity allowing them to retain great power status and useful only so long as it achieved that, for the Communists governing the USSR it was their reason for existence. Once they had dragged Russia out of the feudal age and accelerated it through the capitalist phase via the dictatorship of the proletariat, they would arrive at the socialist utopia outlined by Marx and shaded in by Lenin. The VKP was also fortunate in that the party and the urban workforce wanted change; they welcomed the acceleration of development and did not try to resist it as the peasants had. In fact many of them embraced the idea of creating a 'new Russia'. They felt they were taking part in something both modern and heroic. The problem was that the First World War and then the Civil War reduced the Soviet economy to a shambles. Factories were destroyed, millions were dead, farmland was desolated and society was traumatised. Much of the upper and middle class had fled into exile and the peasantry were unco-operative and hostile. Party control outside the cities had collapsed, peasant armies were creating semi-autonomous zones across the country, territory had been lost (in particular Poland), and the threat of foreign invasion was still high.

The country had to be stabilised before the party could embark on any sustained process of modernisation. This is why Lenin introduced the NEP. The party kept control of the 'commanding heights' of the economy (industrial production) but allowed free market forces to determine food supply and small-scale production. This policy was successful in restoring a measure of stability and prosperity to the country, but was resented by many in the party as unso-cialist, a retreat from the revolutionary aspirations of 1917. Under the NEP about 80% of small-scale production and 99% of farming remained in the private sector. The NEP had restored industrial output and investment to 1913 levels by 1927 but more than a million urban workers were unemployed. Peasants, small-scale businesses and the traders known as NEP-men ensured that a private commercial economy continued to thrive, and this aroused the suspicion and resentment of the Communist Party and its urban supporters. Was this what 1917 had aimed to achieve?

Thus if we look back at pre-Revolutionary Russia we can see why the progress of modernisation and industrialisation was slow. Russian society was semi-feudal and the tsar essentially uninterested in modernising except to preserve his great power status. The tsarist system was traditional, largely rural and based on the twin pillars of political autocracy and religious orthodoxy. Russia had made some steps on the path to modernity by 1914 and the urban centres of Moscow and St Petersburg had seen rapid growth, but taken as a whole Russian society was still backward. Conflict with Germany had destroyed the stability of a society already strained by war and revolt in 1905, peasant and urban unrest in the years that followed, and the pressure for reform from both radical and moderate parties. After 1917 there was little real support for a constitutional monarchy or liberal government from either the urban workers (who favoured the Bolsheviks) or the peasants (who wanted the SRs to take power). Once the Civil War had been resolved and the NEP had restored a degree of economic stability, the party felt confident enough to begin to think about the next stage of action: the final shift to a Communist society and industrialisation. It was motivated by the urge to modernise but also by the desire to achieve a genuinely socialist economy.

The NEP had resulted in a mixed economy. It had been part socialist and part capitalist. In fact, more than 80% of the population (the peasants) remained engaged in private enterprise (selling grain). Many in the party were unhappy about this and wanted to change the Soviet Union to a fully socialist economy. However, there was still a lot of disagreement as to how this change would take place. On the left, Trotsky, Kamenev and Zinoviev had been 'ultra-industrialisers' and called for an end to the NEP. Bukharin and his main supporters Alexei Rykov and Mikhail Tomsky had advocated more moderate, gradualist policies that would see the private sector gradually wither away. Stalin had been equivocal about which policy he supported. In the end he out-manoeuvred both groups to position himself as party leader by 1929, but while doing so it seems he had decided to ally himself with the 'leftist' groups in the party and adopt the radical industrialisation policies he had cautioned the party against in 1926–27. By 1925–26 industry had recovered to its pre-1913 levels and there was a feeling that a new impetus was needed to accelerate development. There was also high unemployment among urban workers and a feeling that the NEP was not working for them. The NEP-men were getting rich and the peasants were prospering, but the natural constituency of the VKP, the urban workers, were being left out of the economic recovery of the 1920s. This was exacerbated by the food shortages of 1926 and 1927 which party leaders, especially Stalin, began to feel were attributable to peasants hoarding grain to drive prices up (which was true).

This controversy over the NEP led to the conflict of the 1920s and Stalin's eventual takeover of power. It also led in part to collectivisation, as once Stalin decided the peasantry were opposing him (and thus the party's progress), it became inevitable that some conflict would occur. But Stalin was also leading a drive to force rapid industrialisation. As Party Secretary and a member of the Politburo, the Orgburo and the Secretariat, he had enormous power, and by 1929 he was sufficiently secure in his position to throw his weight behind collectivisation and rapid industrialisation. Both policies were interlinked. Of the two, I would argue that industrialisation was Stalin's priority. Collectivisation was a means to an end. That end was a strong modern Soviet superpower, able to challenge the West and create 'Socialism in One Country'. This was Stalin's 'so-called "socialist offensive", which combined rapid industrialisation with the forcible collectivisation of peasant agriculture' (R. W. Davis). He was also pushing through this policy while the rest of the world was experiencing the Great Depression caused by the collapse of the US stock market in 1929. How did he do this? Literally through blood, sweat and tears. A US specialist working in Magnitogorsk reckoned that more people died creating this new city than at the Battle of the Marne in 1914.

Industrialisation was also more of a rational policy than collectivisation. Alan Bullock states, 'The industrialisation of Russia was clearly more of an economic success than the collectivisation of agriculture', but he adds, 'How much, if anything it owed to the latter is a matter of debate.' Industrialisation, he believes, could have been achieved without collectivisation. The argument for starving the peasantry to fund collectivisation was the brainchild of the economist Preobrazhensky, but by 1930–31 agriculture was so crippled that even though procurements remained stable they did not generate much capital. This assertion remains unproven; the linkage between collectivisation and industrialisation is a difficult one to debate. Was there a viable alternative in 1929 to the path the party took? The VKP leadership was limited in its options: it had to modernise with minimal capital, surrounded by hostile powers and with decades of neglect and war to contend with. There was also an almost automatic tendency to pursue radical solutions.

Centralised plans

Stalin's decision to push through industrialisation was a response to what he saw as an economy in crisis. The NEP had failed to destroy the private sector (and in fact had encouraged it) and the economy was at a crossroads, as by 1927 it had achieved pre-1914 levels of output and was now stalling. In addition it seemed some kind of grain crisis was materialising. Stalin decided that a centralised push was needed to accelerate growth. Essentially modernisation would have to be imposed from above. The central problem of how to deal with the fact that so many peasants remained was to be solved by collectivisation, and the VKP could then push through industrialisation. This strategy was achieved at heavy cost. It has been estimated that by 1937 total industrial production was four times that of 1928. How in reality was this achieved?

It is worth stating at the start of any examination of the effects of the Five-Year Plans that what was achieved was extraordinary. Even allowing for propaganda and government exaggeration, the increases in output in major industries were astonishing. This is even more striking when it is remembered that the rest of the world was languishing in the economic doldrums as a result of the Great Depression of 1929. Some examples will suffice to show the incredible achievements of the Five-Year Plans. Crude oil production rose from 11.6 million tons in 1928 to 27.4 million tons by 1936. Electric power increased from 18 million kWh in 1927 to 90 million kWh by 1940. Coal production rose from 35.5 million tons a year in 1928 to 150 million tons by 1940.

Stalin announced the start of the First Five-Year Plan at the Fifteenth Party Congress in December 1927. High targets were set for industry, the NEP was abandoned and there was to be limited collectivisation (about 20% of peasant households). The party, frightened by a deterioration in relations with Poland, Britain and France and worried about a resurgent Japan, welcomed this 'left turn'. The fear of war made industrial development imperative. The Great Turn, the shift from the NEP to collectivisation and industrialisation, created a 'command economy' (in which the state decided all economic matters, from prices to the amounts of goods produced) supported by socialised agriculture. Industrialisation would increase the proletariat, lead to an urbanised and literate society, and expand industrial production to allow the Soviet regime to compete with the West. These aims were all rational and to a large extent had been party policy since Lenin. What was new was the rate of change and the ruthlessness Stalin showed in making the transition. Also new was the level of interference in the economy, which would become a fact of life in this new phase of Soviet development. The government was going to take over the planning of all goods and labour. This would obviously require a large state bureaucracy, but it would also lead to confusion, replication and (because of the terrible sanctions for failure) a high degree of chaos as those under Stalin attempted to meet his targets.

In fact this state-led construction of an industrial economy was not really Marxist at all. Marx had envisaged society progressing to communism after having passed through the industrial/capitalist phase. Stalin (like Lenin before him) was happy to subscribe to the view that the Soviet state could leapfrog this phase of economic development under the dictatorship of the proletariat. Capitalist encirclement had also not been foreseen by Marx, who believed that the Communist revolution was inevitable at a certain stage of capitalist development. Stalin's 'Socialism in One Country' was not a necessity that Marx would have prophesied. The idea that the USSR would have to go it alone while the states surrounding it remained capitalist was one that party leaders had to adapt to in the 1920s as they realised that Europe was not going to fall to communism. This led to a further emphasis on military development, which Marx had also not accounted for.

The Five-Year Plans were ambitious. In total there were three of them. The First Five-Year Plan, announced at the end of 1927, really only began in October 1928 and was supposedly finished by 1932 (effectively a year early, even though none of its targets was reached). The Second Five-Year Plan officially started in January 1933 but did not get underway until January 1934, as a year was taken up by deciding targets and quarrelling between the different agencies. This plan is generally accepted to have lasted until December 1937 (so in reality it was 4 years long) and has been seen as the most stable and successful in achieving its targets. In 1937–38 problems emerged: the economy stagnated, harvests were poor and war looked increasingly likely. This was also the period when the Terror was in full swing and experts at all levels of society from engineering to the military were disappearing into the gulag. The Third Five-Year Plan was scheduled to start in late 1937 and run to the end of 1942. The NKVD (the new name for the Soviet secret police, previously known as OGPU) arrested many of the financial planners at Gosplan in this period and shattered morale, which only began to recover from January 1938. However, the invasion of Hitler's armies in June 1941 abruptly terminated this third plan and the economy shifted into coping with the demands of 'total war'. Thus the Third Five-Year Plan was the shortest; effectively lasting from January 1938 to June 1941.

What did the leaders of the USSR hope to achieve in these plans (called *pyatiletki* in Russian)? Basically they wanted to transform the USSR into a modern industrial state. The problem was that in 1927 the USSR was a long way from this. In fact it was predominantly an agrarian society with a small urban population and a relatively weak governmental infrastructure. The leadership, however, was determined to change this and there was popular enthusiasm for them. One Komsomol (Young Communist league) leader remembered welcoming the chance to work in the 'shock brigades' in the factories. He recalled:

> When we went to work in the factories, we lamented that there was nothing left for us to do, because the revolution was over, because the severe but romantic years of civil war would not come back, and because the older generation had left to our lot a boring, prosaic life that was devoid of struggle and excitement.

Lev Kopelev remembers that 'factories, mines, blast furnaces, locomotives, tractors, work-benches, turbines were transformed into objects of a cult'. Alexander Avdeyenko, a Donbass steelworker in the 1920s, saw a propaganda poster at a railway station that motivated him to volunteer for these shock brigades: 'It was of the world, shackled in chains which encircled it. Smashing the chains was a blacksmith — a Soviet blacksmith. I wanted to be that blacksmith.'

Avdeyenko went to Magnitogorsk (a gigantic city of blast-furnaces, factories and iron smelting being built in the 1930s) and was soon at work. He recalls:

> I drove a railway track engine. It was small and powerful and very beautiful. I was very proud of it. It was very useful to Magnitogorsk, carrying the molten metal in eight-ton hoppers, six or eight at a time. I blew the whistle as much as possible. I didn't have to but I wanted to. I was building the heartland of socialism.

This popular enthusiasm, this patriotic outpouring, was one of the reasons for the plan's success. Magnitogorsk is a good case study exemplifying the nature of the Five-Year Plans and the industrialisation of the Soviet Union. Magnitogorsk was near the southern tip of the Urals on 'magnetic mountain', with huge iron ore reserves. Although it was a traditional industrial area, the decision to create a super-city was an exercise in socialist planning and propaganda. Magnitogorsk was going to be an example of the new society created by 'socialist' man. We know so much about it because an American, John Scott, worked there from 1932 to 1942 and wrote a book, *Behind the Urals*, about it. Broadly sympathetic to the project, the book nonetheless gives us a vivid account of how the Soviets carved a city out of nothing, and of the terrible cost to many of the workers taking part in this enterprise.

The creation of Magnitogorsk was part of a general belief in new socialist planning principles. In 1929 a national construction programme named the 'General Plan for Building Socialism' was created. It aimed to build a number of new cities of about 60,000 inhabitants in important economic and industrial zones. Stalingrad was one example of this. It was decentralised, stretching 64 kilometres along the Volga (something the Wehrmacht would be only too well aware of in 1942). Housing in these new cities was to be communal; there would be plenty of parkland and woods and impressive communal buildings (town halls and the like) celebrating the socialist achievements of the age. Magnitogorsk, as Richard Overy states, was to be 'the jewel in the architectural crown of the new Communist order'. By the time it was completed, it would be home to more than 200,000 people and a showpiece of the new Stalinist age. During much of its construction, though, it resembled a war zone, with workers living in primitive conditions. There was a cavalier attitude to worker safety, and heavy casualties. Workers were to be housed in giant high-rise buildings called 'super blocks', intended to be models of socialist living, with everyone sharing communal spaces and surrounding green parkland. At the time they were hardly models of architectural excellence. The first super block was finished in 1933 and lacked toilets or any functioning sanitation. The second was completed in 1937 but was too unsafe to live in, so most workers lived in shacks clustered around the factories (much as they would have done a hundred years before). The Soviet regime's vision of its new cities was utopian: workers' cities where conditions would cause envy among those labouring in the capitalist world. Unfortunately, as is so often the case when the state organises everything, the vision was far from the reality. Nonetheless the creation of Magnitogorsk is testimony to the determination and will of the Soviet leadership and people to modernise, whatever the cost.

Who was in charge?

It was all very well for Stalin to decree a transformation of Soviet industry, but how did this actually occur? There were a number of organisations whose job it was to plan the Soviet economy. Gosplan had been set up in February 1921 to help coordinate initial plans to electrify and industrialise the USSR and to sort out the economy. From 1925 it published annual economic reports. These always included 'control figures' predicting growth for the next year. Gosplan was essentially a small team of economists that expanded its activities over the following 2 years to include drawing up annual plans and future Five-Year Plans. Gosplan was linked to (but really under the ultimate control of) the Supreme Council of the National Economy (VSNKh, pronounced 'Vesenkha'). This body was made up of the party chiefs and so was also involved in planning future economic development.

Individuals were also important. One of the best known was Yevgeny Preobrazhensky, who had published an article entitled 'The Fundamental Law of Socialist Accumulation' in August 1924. Preobrazhensky believed that 'primitive socialist accumulation' (squeezing the peasants to pay for the cities) was the answer to the problem of how the USSR could afford to modernise. If the government procured cheap grain from the peasants and sold it expensively to urban workers of foreign countries, it could create a surplus that could be invested in the nation's industry. Trotsky had also supported this view and as head of the War Commission had decided that the peasants should pay for industrial development. At this time supporters of the NEP had managed to persuade the greater part of the party to hold firm and avoid this path, but the grain crises led to growing support for more radical measures.

Stalin's position at this stage was still equivocal. At the Fourteenth Party Congress in 1925 he had supported calls for modernisation, but in February 1926 in his pamphlet *Concerning Questions of Leninism* he was still arguing that to catch up with the West it would be necessary to increase the living standards of both the rural and urban classes. However, he was beginning to switch emphasis, with support from his close colleagues Valerian Kuibyshev (later head of VSNKh and Gosplan) and Sergo Ordzhonikidze, who became the People's Commissar for Heavy Industry and effectively directed the First Five-Year Plan. By the Fifteenth Party Congress in December 1927, Stalin had shifted in favour of rapid modernisation and announced the First Five-Year Plan. No fewer than seven of the Congress's 29 sessions were given over to examining Gosplan and VSNKh's plans for future development. No detailed directives emerged, but some big industrial projects were already in progress: the Volga-Don canal, the Dneprostroy hydroelectric complex in the Ukraine, and the Turksib railway link between Turkestan's cotton fields and Siberia's grain and timber mills. The debate over how much investment was necessary for successful industrialisation was well underway. In 1926–27 investments in new enterprises doubled and there were demands for a further 25% increase in capital investment in 1928–29. So even while the debate proceeded, the issue was being decided on the ground by the leadership's support and demand for increased capital investment. Not to be outdone, Gosplan matched VSNKh's demands for investment and wild projections of potential success. The matter was given extra importance by the Shakhty Affair trial in March 1929, in which 55 engineers at the Donbass mines were accused of 'sabotage' and 'wrecking' in collusion with unnamed foreign powers. This was the first of many show trials, where fantastical charges were brought against innocent bureaucrats. They led to the dismissal of many technicians and scientists and a wave of 'specialist-baiting', in which proletarian shock brigades were brought in to shake up factories and industrial plants. The party also announced it was training Communists to study engineering and increase workers' technical education.

In 1927 VSNKh and Gosplan drafted instructions for the First Five-Year Plan. The first draft was 740 pages, but the final version stretched to 2,000 pages and contained more than 340 pages of statistics. It was snappily titled the 'Five-Year

Plan for National Economic Construction'. It laid down very ambitious targets. Pig iron output, for example, was to be raised from 3.3 million to 10 million tons per year. Output of coal was to expand from 35.4 million tons to 75 million tons, and that of iron ore from 5.7 to 19 million tons. Light industry would expand by 70%, national income by 103%, agricultural production by 55% and labour productivity by 110%. The annual rate of investment would reach 23.8% by 1932–33. The scale of these targets caught even the most enthusiastic delegates off guard. Added to this was the practical problem of how they were to be achieved. Stalin was typically forthright on the subject, declaring that these targets were 'instructions which are compulsory'.

The First Five-Year Plan

How was the First Five-Year Plan to be achieved? The brief answer is through a combination of raising capital by grain procurements and a campaign of hysterical centralist planning. Targets were set for factories, and when these were achieved they were often doubled or tripled. Huge projects (such as Magnitogorsk) were set in motion across the USSR. A range of special incentives and penalties galvanised workers to work harder and achieve their targets. The working week was extended, the working day lengthened, holidays cut. Absenteeism and lateness became criminal offences. Shock brigades and 'work cadres' of highly paid and motivated workers were sent into factories to increase production, expand norms and generally show everyone else how it was done. The OGPU became involved both in putting the kulaks to work and in rounding up recalcitrant industrial labourers. This was not yet the years of the Terror (1934 onwards), but it was nonetheless a time of repression.

Once the plan was underway a complex series of organisations was charged with securing its success. The most important aspect of the plan was setting production targets and ensuring that they were met. Gosplan and the VSNKh had agreed an 'optimum variant' that outlined the overall direction and ultimate targets, but these were under constant revision. There were also annual and even quarterly targets for specific industries and products. Failure to meet targets could result in sacking, or worse, as the process was gradually criminalised to the point where this failure could be deemed 'wrecking'. Conversely, workers and factories exceeding their targets would receive extra pay and perks.

While the key targets were set by central party organisations such as Gosplan, the business of ensuring the targets were actually met was put in the hands of the People's Commissariats. These Commissariats, the equivalents of government ministries, worked out how to adapt the plan for their region and/or industry. There were four main ones in this period: the Commissariat for Heavy Industry, the Commissariat for Light Industry, the Commissariat for Timber and the Commissariat for Food. Not surprisingly, there was quite a lot of in-fighting and competition for workers and resources between these Commissariats. Stalin relied on his favourite, the brash Sergo Ordzhonikidze, to push the plan through. Ordzhonikidze was first the chairman of the Workers' and Peasants' Inspectorate from 1927 to 1930, then he became head of the VSNKh, and finally in 1932 he was appointed the Commissar of Heavy Industry. By 1939 the number of commissariats had expanded to 20, and this created a host of new problems in terms of competition for resources.

The Commissariat set specific output targets and issued details of what supplies were needed and how much should be paid for materials and wages. The Commissariat would often deal directly with the factory concerned, giving it specific instructions. In other cases it would delegate responsibility to regional administrators who served as the link between the Commissariat and the various factories and companies concerned. These regional administrators might end up effectively being responsible for a whole republic or local authority. The factory director was at the end of this chain and basically had to meet his target or suffer the consequences (which became increasingly unpleasant as the 1930s progressed). In this system decisions were made at the top and emanated from the centre of government. At each level an individual became responsible for ensuring that targets were reached. The problem was that while all these different groups were in charge of fulfilling quotas that required cooperation, the system effectively rewarded them only for achieving their own goals. If you were the manager of a steel plant and needed more iron ore in order to fulfil your production quota, you had to contact the iron ore producer, coordinate with the railways and then organise the smelting of the steel. This was a confusing and complicated process that could be further confused when a senior local party leader decided that something had to be done immediately.

As the confusion spread, Stalin tried to streamline the planning process. Gosplan was 'purged' and reorganised into 11 divisions in 1931. An All-Union Planning Academy was created to educate a new breed of technocrats to run the Plans. In 1935 Gosplan was again reorganised: this time five national departments for overall planning were set up, with a further 16 subdivisions for regional economic planning. In 1932 the VSNKh was abolished and the Politburo took over the overall running of the Plan, and in 1934 an organisation entitled the Control Commission was set up to oversee all aspects of industrialisation. With all these changes and new organisations being set up, and with a steady stream of experts being sent to the prison camps of the gulag, it is unsurprising that there was a large degree of economic dislocation and confusion.

Another consequence was that the emphasis on heavy industry in the First Five-Year Plan led to the collapse of the trade in consumer goods. Quite simply, there was no funding available to produce goods such as shoes and clothes, and many of the small-scale local factories that had survived until 1928–29 went bust. At the same time, the collectivisation of the peasants had ruined many of the small-scale craft and manufacturing industries that could have made up this shortfall. For many Soviet citizens the 1930s were a time of privation, food shortages and a lack of consumer goods. Nevertheless, by June 1930 the plan was already being hailed as a success. Ordzhonikidze was talking about the plan being completed ahead of schedule, and with typical Stalinist aplomb it was announced that the First Five-Year Plan had been achieved by December 1932. None of its official targets had been achieved, but advances had been made and they were impressive. The official Soviet figures issued at the time were often doctored, so it is difficult to quantify exactly how much had really been achieved, but a lot had certainly been done. Regions such as the Urals, the Kuzbass, the Volga district and the Ukraine saw hundreds of new factories and industrial enterprises springing up, and while many were in the west, Stalin had with some prescience focused much of the development further east, away from the strategically vulnerable borders with the USSR's potential enemies. In republics scarcely touched by modernisation the sudden appearance of factories and industrial complexes transformed local landscapes and societies. Needless to say, the haste of much of this work resulted in mistakes and bad building work, not to mention a general lack of aesthetic consideration in urban planning, but this was not a priority at the time.

The sheer speed of development was causing chaos. It is estimated that the urban population of the USSR was increasing at a rate of 50,000 a week. Millions of peasants flooded in from the countryside as the dislocation of collectivisation forced them off the land. The urban infrastructures often could not cope, and a rash of temporary shantytown dwellings spread. The railway network struggled to cope with the volume of its traffic: raw materials to factories, finished goods to towns, workers to cities. Along with development came the normal tensions of modernisation. Workers moved from job to job in search of better wages, work targets were unrealisable and results were forged, peasants newly arrived from the countryside could not cope with factory life or modern technology and breakages were commonplace. Food was in short supply as a result of collectivisation, and rationing became commonplace in 1932–33. Inflation soared as demand for goods increased, and the government found itself desperately trying to control the forces it had unleashed. The country was being transformed, but the process of transformation was throwing up all sorts of problems that the party was finding it difficult to manage.

As well as the success stories of industrialisation, the Stalinist showpieces, there were the failures and the follies. Stalin has been accused of 'gigantism' (the desire to make each project larger and more spectacular than the last, whatever the rationale). An example of this was the Baltic–White Sea Canal (named the Belomor Canal by the party). This was a 227-kilometre canal linking the two seas and was conceived by Stalin as an opportunity to open up the interior to shipping and trade. It was begun in December 1931 and was totally under the control of the OGPU. At times up to 300,000 prisoners from the gulag system were forced to labour on it, entirely without the help of modern machinery. It was literally carved out of the rock by hand. Estimates of how many died vary, but the number certainly ran into tens of thousands (Robert Conquest quotes the figure of up to 200,000). The canal was too shallow for many ships to navigate and was bombed by the Germans early in the Second World War, becoming virtually unusable. This was a typical Stalinist project: large in conception, involving legions of slave-labourers and designed to reflect his glory as much as to serve an economic purpose. Projects like this might not necessarily have made economic sense, but who was going to tell Stalin he was wrong?

So, to summarise the First Five-Year Plan, we can say it combined various factors. First, a number of planning agencies were involved (such as Gosplan and the VSNKh). The economic rationale behind it had been worked out by socialist economic planners, most notably Yevgeny Preobrazhensky, but with adjustments from others (including Stalin himself). Second, it was closely linked to collectivisation, which effectively meant that the First Five-Year Plan (1928–33) took place against a background of rural chaos and food shortages. Third, the implementation of the plan was confused, with central directives issued by Gosplan circulated to local parties and factories and then implemented without regard to the feasibility of achieving them. Fourth, the Five-Year Plan involved a number of associated projects such as hydroelectric dams, canals and new cities, which required (as did many of Stalin's economic projects) a large degree of slave labour. From 1928 to 1932 this was mainly found from among the ex-kulaks and other peasants caught up in the collectivisation drives. From 1932 onwards it included increasing numbers of party members and petty criminals, and in 1937–38, at the height of the Terror, whole sections of society found themselves sentenced to years in the camps for various crimes. Once the war started there was a new influx, but by this stage the Third Five-Year Plan had been cut short by the German invasion. Finally, the Five-Year Plan was carried out with a high degree of idealism, supported by party cadres, shock brigades and various other elite groups which were brought in to increase production and raise the tempo. Although there was an initial wave of 'anti-specialism', this decreased as Stalin accepted the need for technical expertise to help him with his plans.

How successful was the First Five-Year Plan?

Assessments are difficult, as the official figures are suspect. The output targets and quantities were massaged at all levels by local officials, as no one wanted to be accused of lagging behind or to face the even more dangerous charges of 'wrecking' or sabotage, which could result in hefty prison terms and later execution. Official Soviet figures register an increase in industrial production between 1928 and 1940 of 852%, but most historians consider this highly unlikely. A 1972 Soviet handbook asserted that between 1928 and 1940 Group A industries showed the greatest increase. Group A products were heavy industry products such as coal, oil and steel. Oil production increased from 11.6 to 31.3 million tons, coal from 35.5 to 165.9 million tons, steel from 4.3 to 18.3 million tons, and electricity generation from 5 billion to 48.3 billion kilowatt-hours. Light industry (Group B products, such as consumer goods) showed a much more gradual increase. For example, production of cotton cloth rose from 2,700 million to 4,000 million square metres. These figures cover all three Five-Year Plans, so it is difficult to untangle how much was achieved in these industries in the first one.

The First Five-Year Plan had been designed to expand the coal, iron, steel and other heavy industries. The idea was that this would create a platform from which the Soviet Union could develop further. It would allow the country to cut imports from the West and develop its own technically advanced workforce. The government focused 80% of its investment on heavy industry and opened 1,500 new plants. Electricity generation trebled, coal and iron output doubled, engineering developed and huge new industrial complexes were built. However, this was achieved by sacrificing consumer goods, driving small businesses to the wall and setting up various competing agencies that complicated the fulfilment of quotas. The new workforce pouring into the cities from the countryside was untrained and often caused problems, as it didn't understand how to operate complex machinery. By 1932 the industrial workforce was double that of 1928 and industrial output was growing at 10% a year. Whatever criticisms, problems and confusion the First Five-Year Plan had created, it had been successful in achieving an impressive rate of economic growth. Overall, as Alan Wood states, 'There was no denying the fact that the foundations had been well and truly laid for the transformation of the USSR into an industrial giant.'

The First Five-Year Plan had also succeeded in eliminating the private ownership of land and trade. Collectivisation had destroyed the rural private economy, and the focus on heavy industry had driven many small-scale businesses (particularly in the consumer sector) to bankruptcy. The sectors that had survived (and even thrived) under the NEP had been brought under state control. By 1937, 93% of all peasant households were in the state sector. However, the sheer scale of the undertaking and the stresses involved had shaken the party. According to Chris Ward:

> Breakneck industrialisation caused enormous social strains and vast economic dislocations — so much so that in 1932–33 the entire experiment teetered on the verge of collapse. Costs were running far in excess of GOSPLAN's predictions and sudden bottlenecks appeared everywhere…the resultant pressure on housing, transport and social services was colossal.

The pressures of the plan had also affected the leadership of the party. Simon Sebag Montefiore writes:

> By the summer (of 1933) the magnates were exhausted after 5 years of Herculean labour…after bearing such strain they needed to relax if they were not going to crack…Comrade Sergo…suffered heart and circulatory complaints…Kirov was also breaking under the pressure, suffering from 'irregular heartbeat…severe irritability and very poor sleep'. The doctors ordered him to rest. Kirov's friend Kuibyshev, GOSPLAN's boss, who had the impossible task of making the planning figures work, was drinking and chasing women!

If the party leadership was reacting to the pressure being heaped upon them in this way, imagine the effect on the wider Soviet society. Probably the most stressful positions were those occupied by middle-management bureaucrats in charge of factories or regional organisations. Faced with impossible targets and the threat of being accused of wrecking or sabotage if they failed to meet their quotas, they were under constant pressure. It was this group of committed party bureaucrats who would suffer so terribly in the purges to come in the period from 1934 onwards. Yevgenia Ginzburg captures their plight very movingly in her book, *Journey into the Whirlwind*. She and her husband, both middle-ranking party officials in regional offices, loyal activists who had helped the collectivisation drive and joined the 'twenty-five thousanders' who had helped root out peasants' grain and force them into the collective farms, were both later arrested on trumped-up charges of espionage and anti-party activity and sent to the gulag.

The pressure can be seen, for example, in the way targets in the First Five-Year Plan for the production of pig iron were repeatedly and radically shifted upwards from year to year. In 1928 the target was 656,000 tons per year. By the summer of 1929 this had been upgraded to 850,000 tons. By the end of the same year 1,100,000 tons were being demanded, and by early 1930 this had more than doubled to 2,500,000 tons. Clearly, meeting such targets was virtually impossible, and a whole host of measures was adopted to avoid trouble. The obvious tactic was to lie and simply report that you had produced more than you had (this involved an element of cooperation with the next level up and thus created the later 'conspiracies' uncovered by the party). A far easier response was simply to produce poor-grade products (whatever they were) and pass them on to the next link in the chain. Thus the production facilities that needed pig iron received poor-quality material that they had little choice but to use. The lack of detailed planning needed to coordinate such a vast enterprise meant that many of the targets effectively existed only in the realms of fantasy. Some factories overproduced, some underproduced, and many produced sub-standard goods that were virtually useless.

The fears of managers that failure would result in stiff prison sentences or even death were not unfounded. The Shakhty coal mines in the Donbass region had been investigated by the OGPU, and various staff members had been accused of counter-revolutionary activities. Five were executed and others were sentenced to long prison terms. In April 1929 Stalin stated:

Shakhtyites are now ensconced in every branch of our industry…by no means all have been caught. Wrecking by the bourgeoisie intelligentsia is one of the most dangerous forces of opposition to developing socialism, all the more dangerous in that it is connected with international capitalism. The capitalists have by no means laid down their arms; they are massing for new attacks on the Soviet government.

Further trials were concocted to demonstrate that problems in the First Five-Year Plan could be pinned on anti-Communist agents working in league with various enemies. In November 1930 another show trial convened to judge the activities of the so-called Industrial Party. Again the accused were high- and middle-ranking bureaucrats and industrialists accused of counter-revolutionary activity and of wrecking the Five-Year Plans. Eight leading metropolitan engineers and physicists were arrested and charged with various anti-state crimes. The Industrial Party trial was meant to show that Stalin was correct. The leader of the alleged conspiracy was a Professor Ramzin, who was supposed to have been wrecking industry on the orders of the former French President Poincaré and even Lawrence of Arabia and 'other enemies of the Soviet people'. Despite the obviously false nature of the charges, five of the eight charged were sentenced to death (commuted to life imprisonment).

In March 1931 another so-called conspiracy was discovered, this time involving a group of former Mensheviks. They were accused of setting up a 'Union Bureau' to sabotage economic development and of forming a secret bloc with the Industrial Party. Those charged were either summarily shot or disappeared into the labour camps.

Thus in the background of industrialisation there was a very real threat of punishment if plans were not met. However, at this stage Stalin still retained a degree of pragmatism and refused to allow the campaign against specialists to turn into a full-blown cultural revolution. He admitted in June 1931, 'It would be wrong and unwise to regard practically every expert and engineer of the old school as an undetected criminal and wrecker. We have always regarded and still regard "expert-baiting" as a harmful and disgraceful phenomenon.' This did not prevent further trials, such as that of six British Metro-Vickers engineers and ten Soviet technicians in January 1933 for sabotaging power stations. These tactics were typical of Stalin and had already been seen in his March 1930 'Dizzy with Success' speech regarding the collectivisation process. Stalin would condone a general policy of repression that unleashed mayhem, and then in a breathtaking about-turn would condemn these 'excesses' and promise to stop them. This would result in a temporary relaxation of repression before he again unleashed the OGPU and later the NKVD against groups he believed were trying to hinder his policies.

In fact, problems caused by central government's shifting priorities and the general chaos of the plans often resulted in criminal trials. Imaginary campaigns of sabotage met with swift reprisals from the state. As well as the show trials already mentioned, there were several campaigns against 'speculators' and 'wreckers' that resulted in widespread arrests. In the late 1920s party official Georgi Piatakov expressed the view that the problems of the shortage of consumer goods and excessive money supply could be solved by the conventional methods of increasing production, importing fewer consumer goods and exporting agricultural produce. Stalin refused to accept this and stated that confiscating coins from 'speculators', who kept small change because the silver content exceeded its nominal value, could reduce the money supply. Stalin ordered, 'Without fail shoot two or three dozen wreckers from the Commissariat of Finance and the State Bank.' As a result, five bankers were sentenced to death, but were spared when the protests of the poet Osip Mandelstam resulted in a rare moment of amnesty. Stalin fired Georgi Piatakov and continued with his repressive measures. Piatakov himself was later accused of conspiracy, sentenced to death and executed. The sinister threat of arrest, imprisonment and execution that ran through this period is an important factor in assessing how the targets in the first Five-Year Plans were met and why official figures cannot necessarily be trusted.

By 1933 the Soviet Union had undergone radical transformation. The First Five-Year Plan and the collectivisation drive had created enormous changes. The peasants had borne the brunt of the suffering and the so-called kulak class had been effectively destroyed. The gulag system had expanded hugely and was now an integral part of the economic and social structure of the Soviet Union. There would be, as Solzhenitsyn notes, constant new influxes of inmates as Stalin purged various sections of Soviet society. First kulaks, then party members, then the military and lastly prisoners of war and entire ethnic groups suspected by Stalin of treachery in the war. Soviet industry had been massively expanded and the foundations laid for the shift to a modern industrial state. As a by-product of collectivisation the countryside had been depopulated as millions of dispossessed peasants flooded into the growing cities, which obviously helped the process of urbanisation.

There had been profound changes in Soviet society. In 1933, 43% of the 3.5 million party members were what we would call white-collar workers (working in an office). A few years before, the figure had been only 8%. Between January 1930 and October 1933, 660,000 workers in the party had been moved from the factory floor into administrative, educational or political work. Technical institutes were created to train a new breed of Soviet administrators, many of whom had never been to secondary school. The future premier Nikita Khrushchev, for example, entered the Moscow Industrial Academy in 1929 when he was 35 years old. This party elite received better pay, working conditions, housing and holiday opportunities. In fact the state became the largest employer in the Soviet Union. In 1928, 11.4 million people worked in state enterprises. By 1932–33 the total was 22.8 million. This growth slowed in the second and third plans (by 1940, 31.2 million people worked in state enterprises). The country underwent growing urbanisation: between 1926 and 1939 the urban population rose by about 30 million, including many peasants (some estimates put the number as high as 18.5 million). Living conditions were consequently often basic and overcrowded, with food and consumer goods in short supply. In many ways the experience of this period was typical of that of any society undergoing its first and most intense stage of industrial development. The main difference in the USSR was the speed with which this process was occurring.

Alongside all this change and danger there was also opportunity. Skilled workers were needed and were in short supply. In July 1930 Kuibyshev bemoaned 'the shortage of trained and educated personnel'. The party was trying to rectify this shortage by setting up technical colleges, importing foreign specialists and promoting party members, but there was still a skills gap. The party also wanted to ensure the loyalty of this new breed of technical specialists. In 1927 only 2.1% of Soviet engineers were in the party, and this worried the leadership. The new technocrats would be party members through and through. A wave of worker enthusiasm for industrialisation had led to specialist-baiting and general distrust of 'former bosses and capitalists' who still retained their positions. Stalin had to some extent encouraged this bad feeling, seeing it as a way to harness the energy of the working class, but had had to limit it when it threatened the success of the plans. Production communes, shock brigades, Komsomol 'light cavalry detachments' and other militaristic workers' groups had mobilised the urban workers, but they also caused chaos in some factories as managers struggled against charges of being 'bourgeois sympathisers'. This tension remained throughout the 1930s but died down after the initial frantic mobilisations of 1928–30.

The events of 1928–33, both collectivisation and the First Five-Year Plan, had cemented Stalin's control of the USSR. All power in the Soviet Communist Party's four organs — the Politburo, the Secretariat, the Orgburo and the Central Control Commission — was in his hands. The Council of People's Commissars (the Sovnarkom) and the Workers' and Peasants' Inspectorate were run by trusted lieutenants. Kalinin was the head of state, and although he was the last remaining leader to have been appointed in Lenin's time, he was under firm control. Stalin effectively ruled the Soviet Union alone and with the help of his committed team of cronies (the likes of Kaganovich, Ordzhonikidze and Molotov) from the Kremlin. Stalin could rely on OGPU support to back up his policies with terror. The Soviet Union in 1934, although not yet in the state of abject fear and paranoia into which it descended in 1937–38, was a society cowed and under Stalin's control.

Eliminating dissent

But what should he do now? He had broken the peasantry and pushed through the First Five-Year Plan. The whole process had been immensely traumatic. Millions were dead, and Stalin had been worried about the success of the whole enterprise on more than one occasion (1933 being probably his most stressful time). But the Soviet Union had begun the process of transformation into a modern state of sorts. Productivity in many areas had soared, huge new projects had begun and an increasing degree of urbanisation had been achieved. A growing class of educated party personnel had emerged and was being trained in the expanding technical colleges. Schools were also expanding. In fact 1934 looked like being a good year. Fear of foreign invasion had died away and relations with Britain and France were cordial (even though a new threat was emerging in the form of Hitler). The harvest was good and the cities got more food. OGPU executions were down (2,000 were executed, as opposed to 20,000 in 1931). A record number of 'counter-revolutionaries' had gone to the camps in 1933 (139,000) and more than 62,000 died in the gulag, but these were mainly the last of the peasants deemed to be kulaks and thus their fate was 'invisible' to the workers in the cities. The First Five-Year Plan had been broadly successful; certainly Stalin was hailing it as such. The famine in the Ukraine had been largely unreported, and those in the cities had been shielded from the full horrors of collectivisation.

However, Stalin was not prepared to rest content. Although he had succeeded in consolidating his grip on power and pushing through his radical policies, he still wanted to continue with the drive to industrialise. At the same time another and more deadly preoccupation was emerging. He had broken the peasantry and had demonstrated through his show trials of 1930–33 that he could control society, but the party remained beyond his absolute control. He was effectively dictator of the Soviet Union, but he wanted to make sure that his grip was unchallenged. In 1934 another wave of repression was launched, after a single event whose impact would affect the planned projection of the USSR's economic strength, bring a flood of new inmates to the camps and threaten to destroy the Soviet military in the run-up to the Second World War. On 1 December 1934, Sergei Kirov, Party Secretary in Leningrad and both a favourite of and potential rival to Stalin, was assassinated. Stalin's involvement in the murder has been much debated. There were undoubtedly many suspicious circumstances surrounding the assassination that could implicate Stalin. Whether he was involved or not, he certainly used the assassination to his advantage and further consolidated his power. In the immediate aftermath a new law was passed, allowing the NKVD to execute anyone involved in 'terrorist acts'. The accused in such cases would have no right of appeal; trials could be carried out in 10 days and the death sentence would be carried out as soon as the verdict was decided. This escalation of the terror to include Stalin's own party was new. Now the Bolsheviks themselves were at the mercy of their leader, and even the NKVD was to find itself purged in the mass slaughter of the 1930s. What is amazing about the USSR in this period is that plans for economic progress took place against this steadily escalating wave of arrests and executions unleashed by the Kirov murder.

The purges that took place between 1934 and 1938 fall outside the main focus of this book, but it is helpful to be aware of them as they had an obvious impact on the economic progress made by the USSR in this period. This was particularly true from 1936 onwards, as growing numbers of party members and technocrats were arrested and sent to the camps. The reasons for the purges within the party and society as a whole have been the subject of much debate. Some historians have focused on Stalin and viewed the purges as a calculated campaign to establish himself in sole power and to destroy any vestiges of opposition (this is very much the view of Robert Conquest, for example). Others have seen the purges as a form of civil war within the party, between the central party organisation and the regions, and between the upper echelons and the middle and lower ranks, which spiralled out of control in a wave of denunciations and score-settling (J. Arch Getty is a proponent of this view). Whatever the causes, the terrible atmosphere of panic and fear engendered by the repression in this period obviously impacted on the economic life of the nation and should be borne in mind in any assessment of the Second and Third Five-Year Plans.

The Second and Third Five-Year Plans

Meanwhile, plans continued for the modernisation of the USSR, and the Second Five-Year Plan was launched. This time, targets were revised to more modest levels. The plan was worked out in more detail for each industry and region. The People's Commissariats were better organised and defined after 1934 and were able to give more specific information to the factories and regions under their control. One of the main areas of investment was the railway system, with the aim of increasing the amount of freight that could be transported (one of the chief problems in the First Five-Year Plan had been bottlenecks in the rail system that had prevented supplies being transported effectively). There was also an emphasis on training workers more effectively. In addition to this, many of the factories and schemes started in the First Five-Year Plan now came on stream, increasing productivity enormously. The Soviet Union became almost self-sufficient in machine tools and much less dependent on foreign imports of machinery. In fact the years 1934–37 were in many ways the most successful of the whole period. After 1937 the USSR began to slow down again and the arms industry absorbed increasing amounts of funding. The purges also began to take effect. Economic historian Alec Nove believes they seriously undermined economic progress and began to 'spin out of control', undermining Soviet progress:

> The purge swept away…managers, technicians, statisticians, planners, even foremen. Everywhere there were said to be spies, wreckers, and diversionists. There was a grave shortage of qualified personnel, so the deportation of many thousands of engineers and technologists to distant concentration camps represented a severe loss. But perhaps equally serious was the psychological effect of this terror on the survivors. With any error or accident likely to be attributable to treasonable activities, the simplest thing to do was avoid responsibility, to seek approval from superiors for any act, to obey mechanically any order received, regardless of local conditions.

If this was the case in the free workforce, the idea of achieving economic progress though forced labour was even more unlikely. Solzhenitsyn debates the question of whether the camps justified themselves economically in his book, *The Gulag Archipelago*. He asserts:

> The Archipelago did not pay its own way, and it never will! Here's why. The first and principal cause was the lack of conscientiousness of the prisoners, the negligence of the stupid slaves. Not only could you not expect any socialist self-sacrifice of them, but they didn't manifest simple capitalist diligence. All they were on the look out for was ways to spoil their footgear — and not go out to work; how to break a crane, to buckle a wheel, to break a spade, to sink a pail — anything for a pretext to sit down and smoke. All that the camp inmates did for their dear state was openly and blatantly botched; you could break the bricks they made with your bare hands; the paint would peel off the panels; the plaster would fall off; posts would fall down; tables rock; legs fall out; handles come off. Carelessness and mistakes were everywhere…in the fifties they brought a new Swedish turbine to Steplag. It came in a frame made of logs like a hut. It was winter, and it was cold, and so the cursed *zeks* (prisoners) crawled into this frame between the beams and the turbine and started a bonfire to get warm. The silver soldering on the blades melted — and they threw the turbine out. It cost 3,700,000 roubles…And in the presence of the *zeks* — and this was a second reason — the free employees didn't care either, as though they were working not for themselves but for some stranger or other, and they stole a lot, they stole a great, great deal…the third cause was the *zeks*' lack of independence, their inability to live without jailers…due to all these causes not only does the Archipelago not pay its own way, but the nation had to pay dearly for the additional satisfaction of having it.

But despite the limitations of using slave labour and the effects of the purges from 1937 onwards, in the middle years of the 1930s progress was made. In the Second Five-Year Plan heavy industries still featured strongly, but new industries were developed. The emphasis was on communications linking cities to the new industrial centres. Overall 4,500 enterprises opened. Some of these were big projects, such as the Dneprostroy dam. This period became known as the 'three good years'. Electricity generation expanded rapidly, chemical industries grew, with fertilisers becoming increasingly effective, and minerals such as copper, zinc and tin were mined for the first time. On the negative side, although there had been a promise of expanding consumer goods, in reality investment in them was still low. Expected advances in oil production were also not achieved.

The Third Five-Year Plan was cut short after $3\frac{1}{2}$ years by the German invasion and the outbreak of war. The plan's main focus was on heavy industry and armaments, but overall it was not a great success. Steel output failed to grow, oil production once again failed to meet targets, and there was a fuel crisis. Consumer industries did not receive adequate investment, goods produced were often shoddy, and many factories ran short of materials. The growing threat of war diverted resources and Gosplan was thrown into chaos by the purges. Ward writes:

> After 'three good years', 1937 ushered in a period of drift and stagnation. In the first place, significant distortions appeared as the Politburo, worried by international events, abruptly re-directed large sums to the defence industries. Second, a hard winter in 1937–38 caused drastic fuel shortages, precipitating, on the one hand, severe difficulties in many factories, and on the other renewed crisis on the railways…Third, consumer group investment was once more sacrificed to the insatiable appetites of group A industry. Finally, Stalin's speech at the infamous 1937 February–March plenum, averring to widespread wrecking and sabotage…coupled with the massive purge unleashed by Nikolai Yezhov (head of the NKVD), soon combined to reap a grim harvest of key personnel.

How successful were the Five-Year Plans?

At the Eighteenth Party Congress in March 1939 Molotov felt able to hail the overall success of the previous 10 years of rapid industrialisation. In fact he continued to forecast wildly optimistic figures for future production (gross industrial output was due to rise by 92%). He said he believed that the First and Second Five-Year Plans had laid the foundations for a socialist society; the next 5 years would complete this transition. However, in June 1941 Hitler's Panzers rolled across the border, bringing the third *pyatiletka* to a sudden halt. How should we today view the claims made by the Bolshevik leadership about the success of the plans? Official figures must be viewed with some scepticism. There was also much that was chaotic, badly organised and wasteful about the command economy and the strains it put on the whole of the USSR. Imbalances in the economy, transport problems, bribery and corruption, as well as the pressure to achieve targets whatever the cost, all created big flaws in the system. Consumer goods were in short supply, and even the most basic goods were subject to queues and rationing throughout this period.

But there can be little argument that much was achieved. There was the obvious success of large projects such as Magnitogorsk, the Moscow Metro and the Dnepr Dam, as well as the more dubious achievement of projects such as the Belomor Canal. There was also the enormous expansion in many heavy industries and the growing modernisation of the economy. Certainly the Soviet

Union of 1938 was a very different country to the one inherited by Stalin a decade earlier. Chris Corin and Terry Fiehn write:

> Given the results, some historians have concluded that the type of command economy that emerged, with clearly set priorities, seemed reasonably well suited to the circumstances of the USSR in the 1930s. It got the Soviet industrial juggernaut rolling and that was no mean achievement.

Alan Bullock writes:

> The boldness of the targets, the sacrifices demanded and the vision of what 'backward' Russia might achieve provided an inspiring contrast with an 'advanced' West with millions unemployed and resources left to waste because of the slump. None of Stalin's targets might be achieved, but in every case output was raised: 6 million tons of steel was little more than half the 10 million allowed for, but 50% up on the starting figure.

Looking at the period from a modern perspective, one is tempted to be more circumspect about Stalin's achievements. The terrible cost of collectivisation and the purges must surely temper any positive assessment. Surely nothing can justify the millions that were killed? The whole matter is complicated by the Second World War, which gave Stalinism a retrospective legitimacy — the sacrifices of the 1930s being seen as the price that had to be paid to give Stalin the means to fight Hitler. On the other hand, while this is a difficult point to argue, Stalin almost lost the war in 1941, and how much credit he deserves for the Soviet victory in 1945 is debatable. Modern historians are keen to explore counterfactuals (what-ifs) and ask whether a less destructive path to modernisation could have been followed. Some have looked to the NEP and/or Bukharin as offering a more moderate pathway to modernisation that could have harnessed the enthusiasm of party cadres without needing the gulag. Roy Medvedev and Stephen Cohen, for example, argue that the NEP could have succeeded and that Stalin's policies were wasteful, but R. W. Davis believes that the NEP had run out of steam by 1928–29 and that a gearing-up to a command economy was necessary. Alec Nove also believes that some kind of Stalinist control of the economy was necessary to enable the country to modernise.

Other writers and historians see in the rule of Stalin a 'forgotten holocaust'. Writers such as Donald Rayfield, Martin Amis and Alexander Solzhenitsyn focus on the human tragedy of Stalin's rule. From this perspective it is difficult to assess Stalinism as anything other than a tragedy for the Soviet people. Rayfield writes:

> The Soviet Union and its successor states have never achieved what psychiatrists call closure…today's Russian state refuses to abjure Stalin and his hangmen. Denunciations

have come from either non-governmental organisations — Memorial, the Sakharov centre — or else from men who, like Khrushchev, were up to their neck in blood...Today's secret police, the FSB, take pride in their Cheka ancestry.

Whatever Stalin's achievements in building up the economy, he is irrevocably condemned by his terrible crimes. Historians are accustomed to taking the long view of events, and may be able to weigh up the deaths of millions more neutrally when assessing economic or social advances, but it is difficult to escape the insanity and terrible waste of Stalin's policies, particularly collectivisation.

So what can we conclude about the Five-Year Plans? First, that the party leadership saw them as an essential step towards the success of socialism and communism in the Soviet Union. Second, Stalin also believed they were essential to protect the country from threatening enemies who encircled it and wanted to destroy it. He believed the modernisation of the Soviet Union was imperative if the Communist Party were to avoid the fate of all previous Russian rulers (i.e. defeat by more advanced countries/armies). The Five-Year Plans were initiated from above, but there was a great deal of support for them from rank-and-file party members and urban workers. The Communist Party leadership effectively tapped into a patriotic desire to modernise the Soviet Union and show the West what it was capable of. The Five-Year Plans relied on a command economy with centralised planning and target-setting. These plans and targets were then sent out to factories and regions under the control of the various Commissariats. Although the plans were designed to last 5 years, actual operational targets were adapted yearly and even quarterly. Targets were frequently revised upward and shifted with little warning. The targets were often unrealistic, and some would argue unachievable under any circumstances. They were deliberately inflated in order to drive the workers to attempt to achieve the impossible.

Running the plans was extremely stressful and involved a large degree of state coercion and terror. The show trials of the early 1930s were followed by the purges of the mid-1930s, with the result that middle managers and specialists in particular were kept in a state of fevered intimidation. Under such pressure to achieve overfulfilment of the targets, figures were massaged and results inflated so that officials could secure targets and avoid arrests and other sanctions. Corruption, bribery and inefficiency were all a result of this pressure to produce the quotas whatever the cost, and led to a huge amount of waste being built into the system. The First Five-Year Plan was the most chaotic and in some areas failed to deliver much, as the goods produced were so often faulty and so many mistakes were made. However, despite all these problems heavy industry expanded massively, large-scale projects were undertaken (and completed), and manufacturing potential was increased. There were 'winners' and 'losers' in the Plans. Obvious 'winners' were skilled urban workers who were not too high up in administration. Obvious 'losers' were the peasants and later (ironically) middle management in the party and specialists, who were the very people most needed to fulfil the Plans and yet who fell victim to the purges.

Soviet society underwent radical transformation, but living standards remained low and many workers barely survived on subsistence wages and food. Displaced peasants who moved to the cities to find work fared worst, with little technical expertise and no job security. The introduction of internal passports in 1932 made their lot even harder, as they had to move around constantly to survive.

The Second Five-Year Plan should be seen as the most successful: a large degree of stabilisation occurred, with the most rapid expansion of the economy taking place. From 1937 the purges, the threat of war and general economic stagnation caused the Third Five-Year Plan to founder, and the Nazi invasion in 1941 brought it to an abrupt halt. Overall the Soviet Union advanced rapidly throughout this period, but at a terrible cost in lives and suffering. The gulags and their reserves of slave labour were used to help drive modernisation (although how effectively they did so is a matter of debate, particularly if you look at the criticisms of the system articulated so persuasively by Solzhenitsyn). Whatever their real economic benefit, the party leadership, particularly Stalin, saw the pool of slave labour provided by the camps as essential. There is plenty of evidence for this in his emphasis on quotas to keep the camps full and the use of convicts in dangerous mining and construction projects.

Questions

1 How planned were the Five-Year Plans?

2 What did the Five-Year Plans achieve?

3 How successful were the Five-Year Plans?

Stalin's Soviet Union: a nation transformed?

Collectivisation and the Five-Year Plans clearly had an immeasurable impact on the Soviet Union. Some historians have argued that the period 1928–29 was as important as 1917 in terms of modern turning points in the history of Russia and its empire. Collectivisation certainly changed Russia more profoundly than the October Revolution (although to some extent it was the logical conclusion of a process that began with the storming of the Winter Palace). Stalin had moved the Soviet Union created by Lenin from a primarily peasant-based, backward society to a modern industrial power and one that was well placed (whatever the bungling associated with the Nazi invasion) to resist invasion by the most modern and powerful army in Europe (and possibly the world). Without the industrial base created between 1929 and 1941 it is debatable that the Red Army would ever have been able to muster the resources necessary to defeat the Wehrmacht.

A new Communist society, or an experiment that failed?

But in what other ways was the Soviet Union transformed? Had the social experiment worked? Was there a new breed of superworker? Had *homo sovieticus* emerged to lead the world proletariat to victory? There had certainly been change, but what it was and what it had achieved is open to debate. So far, in looking at events from 1928 to 1941 this book has taken a top-down approach. We discussed the background to collectivisation and the Bolsheviks' relationship with the peasantry. We looked at Lenin's views of what might happen in Russia as it became Communist and how the 'peasant issue' would be dealt with. We focused on Stalin and his rise to power and how he drifted (to some extent) into supporting collectivisation and rapid industrialisation. We examined collectivisation and how and why it was carried out, and tried to assess the cost and any positive conclusions that could be ascribed to it.

We then looked at the rapid industrialisation of the USSR in the 1930s through the Five-Year Plans. This involved considering why Russia had failed to effectively modernise before 1914 and how the war and revolution had set the economy back. The Great Turn in 1928 ushered in a state of rapid change that was linked to collectivisation and the development of the Stalinist dictatorship. When looking at the Five-Year Plans it is necessary to have some idea of how the state worked under Stalin and how the use of terror supported the economic crash course that the Soviet Union underwent.

After looking at the three Five-Year Plans and what they had achieved, we drew some potential conclusions concerning a possible approach to assessing them and raised some important questions. Could the human cost be justified in any way? Why had Stalin embarked on such a radical course of action? Was the Soviet Union genuinely transformed by the modernisation and collectivisation policies, and if so, how? What do modern historians think of the period, and how much is coloured by the Second World War? These are all-important issues and allow us to look at the interplay of Stalin and the Communist Party, conflict with the peasantry and the need to modernise.

It is important to establish to what extent Soviet society was changed 'from the bottom' and thus judge whether we can really talk about the USSR as a nation transformed or not. Was there support for the Five-Year Plans? What impact did collectivisation have on the cities? What was it like to live in Soviet cities? Were there positive aspects in this period? How much was repression a factor? What were the incentives to support Stalin? We have touched on these issues, but any assessment of the Five-Year Plans requires a more detailed look at the life of the workers in the cities and their role in events.

Stalin's main objective was to modernise the USSR and create a Communist society. This would involve transforming a mainly rural agrarian society into a modern industrial state. One part of this process was achieved by collectivisation, which effectively destroyed the independent traditions of the peasantry. Linked to this policy was the rapid industrialisation initiated in the Five-Year Plans. Backing up this whole process were the secret police and the extensive system of labour camps. All of this was achieved in a political system in which Stalin had effectively achieved dictatorial power (although the size and nature of the USSR meant that he was still for many a distant figure).

The Bolshevik leadership began to talk of a new type of citizen, 'Soviet man'. Proletarian, Communist, revolutionary and rational, he (or she) represented the evolution of the Communist ideal: the first generation of Communists, raised exclusively in a Communist state with no memory of pre-1917 society. In 1928 the creation of this 'new man' was still a distant goal. Eighty per cent of Soviet citizens lived on the land and the urban workers were a minority. Few people received education beyond primary school and there was little technical expertise. The Bolsheviks had relied on the urban workers in 1917 as their main source of support. In the Civil War they had recruited their most successful soldiers mainly from the cities, and it was to the urban workers that the party leadership was to turn in 1928 when it launched the First Five-Year Plan to achieve the initial stages of modernisation. In general the urban working class and young people seem to have been genuinely enthusiastic at the start of the First Five-Year Plan. There was a sense of idealism and a feeling that the 'heroic' stage of the revolution would be rekindled in the drive to industrialise. John Scott, the American who was involved in work at Magnitogorsk, testifies to this genuine idealism in his account of the years he spent building this great new city, and there are plenty of workers from the period who recall their enthusiasm for this phase of modernisation.

The workers also believed that they would benefit from the Five-Year Plans. Many felt that they had missed out on the prosperity promised in the 1920s. In fact many felt that NEP-men and the peasantry had benefited at their expense. Real wages had risen slowly under the NEP and there was still widespread unemployment in the cities. There was support from the factory floor for party attacks on specialists — traditional bourgeois engineers and managers (although the party tempered this campaign when it realised it needed the expertise of these people for the Plans to succeed). The VKP leadership tried to create a new class of technical experts and expand education to those traditionally denied it. This often resulted, as in the case of Nikita Khrushchev, in party members in their thirties returning to college. The rush into education was notable in the First Five-Year Plan and was encouraged by the party leadership (although there was some debate on the quality of training and recruits as numbers expanded alarmingly). In 1932 a high point in enrolments was reached, with 295,600 students registered in higher education. Of these, 62,200 were aiming to become agricultural specialists. Figures dropped in later years but still remained high.

There were problems in retaining students: Martin McCauley estimates that up to 70% of students dropped out of courses. Yet overall the figures are impressive. Between 1928 and 1940, 291,100 specialists graduated with engineering and industrial qualifications. A further 103,400 technical students graduated in agriculture. The emphasis on industrial and engineering targets in the Five-Year Plans led to an increased demand for these students and accounted for about a third of all students in higher education. Other popular areas of study were education (which accounted for 42.6% of students in higher education from 1938 to 1940) and medicine (which generally accounted for about 10% of students). Most of those entering higher education were of working-class origin (in fact the Central Committee decreed that 70% of all new entrants to higher education had to be of such origin). This target was rarely reached, and many entrants from so-called 'bourgeois' origins continued to enter the education system. The proportion of women in education expanded rapidly. In 1928 women had occupied only 14% of places in all of higher education, but by the 1930s they made up a quarter of engineering students and a third of agricultural students, and by 1940 40.3% of engineering students.

The party was keen to expand its influence in technical education. In 1928 only 138 graduate engineers were members of the VKP. By 1937 the number had risen to 47,000. In this period the party benefited from the fact that technical experts, teachers and members of the intelligentsia realised the benefits of party membership. Between 1939 and 1941, 70% of new party members were drawn from this section of the workforce. Clearly this social mobility and increased access to education would have a profound effect on Soviet society and help the party in its attempts to shift the emphasis to modern, urban objectives. Alongside the growth of the educated worker, the cult of the proletariat also developed. It was felt that the industrial workers in the factories and new industrial plants were the heroes of the age. This was given increased emphasis by the Stakhanovite cult that developed in the 1930s and was used in government propaganda to inspire and encourage workers in all industries to increase productivity.

On 30 August 1935, Alexei Stakhanov, a pneumatic-pick operator, started his legendary shift. He began at ten o'clock in the morning and in 5 hours of work he cut 102 tons of coal (sixteen times the norm of 6.5 tons per shift). He was hailed as a hero by the VKP and used as an example of what 'revolutionary enthusiasm' could achieve. In fact the whole situation was something of a set-up. Konstantin Petrov, head of the local party at Central Irmino in the Don Basin, needed some good news to give party bosses higher up the chain, as his region was lagging behind its targets. Stakhanov was a good worker and the party decided to set up ideal conditions to enable him to achieve a 'heroic' output. He was given unlimited compressed air, a good pick, two helpers to prop up the shaft as he progressed, and hauliers to take the coal away. The plan worked. After he had finished his shift Stakhanov received extra pay and a new apartment, and was honoured in a special ceremony. Petrov declared his achievement a world record and encouraged other workers in the plant to try to beat it. Within a week two miners had done so, and so began the competitive Stakhanovite movement that spread across Soviet industry.

The reason for the rapid spread was that the story was picked up by Sergo Ordzhonikidze (Commissar for Heavy Industry), and he put Stakhanov on the front page of *Pravda*. He stated, 'In our country, under socialism, heroes of labour must become the most famous.' On 11 September 1935 *Pravda* used the term 'Stakhanovite movement' for the first time, and in November Stalin called for 'Stakhanovism' to spread 'widely and deeply' across the country. This resulted in a national wave of attempts to break productivity records. In Magnitogorsk, for example, V. P. Ogorodnikov was involved in four out of eight record-breaking shifts in a steel mill in the city. He was rewarded with increased pay, a motorbike and a special house. Again he became a well-publicised hero of the revolution. Some of the Stakhanovites went on to write their auto-biographies and became well-known national figures, held up by the authorities as an example to others.

The Stakhanovite movement threw up many problems for managers, though. Workers understandably wanted to be recognised as Stakhanovites and receive rewards, and it was good propaganda to have such workers at your factory. Yet their feats raised productivity quotas even higher, and laid managers open to the charge that they must not have been pushing their workforce hard enough before if they were suddenly able to attain these new targets. It also created tension within the workforce, as those workers who did not achieve these inflated quotas resented those who did, especially as most successful Stakhanovite records involved a 'fix' with special support and artificial conditions created by the managers. The focus on specific workers or industries distorted the overall output and did not necessarily help the managers reach their total output figures.

The Stakhanovite movement was consistent with the general tendency of the party leadership to try to bypass managers and ally with the workers directly to achieve targets. Stalin and other party leaders were suspicious of 'specialists' and came to feel that their drive to modernise the USSR was being hindered by groups of educated middle management and party officials. Stalin repeatedly struck out at these groups when he was frustrated by the apparent lack of progress in a particular area. In the First Five-Year Plan he focused his anger on technicians and engineers who were not party members. The show trials of the period that exposed 'wreckers' and 'saboteurs' with links to Western powers demonstrated his suspicion of these groups. Yet he realised he needed them in order to industrialise, so he held back from more widespread measures. 'Specialist-baiting' was popular with rank-and-file workers and party members, who often resented the better pay and working conditions they enjoyed and who were automatically suspicious of the so-called intelligentsia (or what was left of it: many scientists and academics had already fled the Soviet Union over the previous decade). Stalin had encouraged such sentiments in 1928–29 but realised he was in danger of losing the people he needed for his modernisation plans, so he tried to temper this movement in the early 1930s.

The Stakhanovite movement was fostered by the party as a means of encouraging greater worker productivity and enthusiasm and putting pressure from below on the managers and regional secretaries to fulfil their output targets. It was characteristic of the time and fitted in with a general belief that 'socialist enthusiasm' rather than specialist knowledge was the key to success. The elevation of the worker to the status of hero was part of the party's attempt to push the country towards its Communist future. The focus on 'class origin' when evaluating people was linked to this. The more humble your background the better, and many of the people who thrived in the 1930s were not those in management or the party but younger workers from poor backgrounds who could claim to be genuinely proletarian. In fact as the 1930s wore on, Stalin increasingly focused on the party itself in his paranoia, and after the Kirov murder in 1934 party members found themselves in the firing line. The purges launched in the mid-1930s targeted regional party members, managers and well-educated specialists. In such circumstances it was better not to occupy a position where you would be noticed by the authorities and blamed if things did not go well.

The pressures on managers were immense. For example, a factory manager had many responsibilities. First and most importantly they had targets they had to meet. Then they had increased labour norms: these stipulated the amount of work expected from workers in an average shift. Throughout the period these were increased. In 1936 they went up by 10% and in some industries they were then increased again. Enterprises were also expected to pay for all the materials they needed in the production process: fuel, raw materials and the workers' wages. Initially the state had subsidised these, but from 1936 they were cut and the pressure increased. Also in 1936 rationing ended and there were more consumer goods available. The price of food began to rise and the workers wanted better wages. The managers obviously had to weigh these demands against the other demands placed on them and try to balance the books. In addition to this there was a shortage of labour from 1936 onwards as the huge influx of peasants subsided. The focus on military spending in this period also made life harder for them. By 1940, state spending on the armed forces accounted for 32.5% of the total government budget. The military got priority in the allocation of resources, and the large numbers of young men conscripted into the army reduced the potential labour pool still further. To cap it all there was a general slowdown in the economy from the mid-1930s, which made imports of machinery more difficult and cut overall productivity.

These pressures would have been hard to deal with in normal times, but they acquired a significant extra menace when failure could be met with charges of 'wrecking'. Failure to meet targets, to fulfil unrealistic norms or to balance books could result in a criminal trial and years in the labour camps. During the Stakhanovite campaign frustrated workers prevented from achieving Stakhanovite classification because of a shortage of tools or resources could charge managers with wrecking by 'hindering us from working in a Stakhanovite fashion'. In such times people also had to be very careful what they said. Expressing doubts about central government priorities or targets was a dangerous business and could result in the finger of suspicion being pointed at individuals for 'defeatist' talk and undermining the Five-Year Plans — and could result in a prison sentence. In such an atmosphere it is not surprising that corruption and rule-breaking were rife. For managers, all that was really important was fulfilling the targets to the satisfaction of the higher authorities. They had to keep their workers happy enough to stop them leaving, and they had to achieve their quota. How they did this was unimportant, so managers resorted to bribery in order to get raw materials and better work out of their skilled workers. Figures were fabricated and sent up the chain; quantity was more important than quality. In such a climate it is not surprising that the reality of industrial progress was often very different from the projected image.

This was also the case in the cities. The Five-Year Plans' stated aim was to industrialise and modernise the Soviet Union. However, the focus on heavy industry meant that little was done to raise the standard of living in the urban areas. In general, life for the workers throughout the 1920s and 1930s was poor. In the 1920s, as the Soviet Union recovered from the terrible conflicts it had endured over the previous decade, the NEP did not really increase worker prosperity. As the party abandoned the policy, there was a feeling among the industrial workers that conditions would improve. The obvious notable achievement of the Five-Year Plans was that they ended the misery of unemployment that had affected many in the cities in the late 1920s. But the demands of the Five-Year Plans sidelined workers and put the needs of industry first. Consumer goods became scarce as the small businesses that had survived during the NEP went bankrupt in the 1930s and the state targets failed to account for this sector of the economy. The chaos of collectivisation and state procurements of grain meant that food rationing was introduced. In Moscow and Leningrad meat, fruit and milk consumption decreased by up to two thirds between 1928 and 1933.

Pressure on the cities grew as their population increased. The flood of peasants into the cities put huge pressure on resources. At one stage up to 200,000 people a month were moving from the countryside to the towns. There was no housing for them, and what were in effect shanty towns grew up on the outskirts of all the major cities. Workers were forced to live in barrack blocks or sub-divided apartment blocks where conditions were primitive. Sewerage systems were not built to cope with this influx; the infrastructure of many urban areas degenerated under the pressure of this new wave of migrants and the lack of central government planning or support. Once again the official line maintained by the party was very different from the reality on the ground. The party stated that life was improving and that workers in the 'socialist paradise' that was the USSR were content and lived well. In fact housing was appalling. Between 1914 and 1920 much of the housing stock had been destroyed, and little was done about this in the 1920s. As cities expanded, the pressure increased on what little there was. It has been estimated that the average citizen had 5.88 square metres of living space (and in many cases far less). Andrew Smith, an American who was living in Moscow in 1932, wrote:

> Kuznetsov lived with about 550 others, men and women, in a wooden structure about 800 feet long and fifteen feet wide. The room contained approximately 500 narrow beds, covered with mattresses filled with straw or dried leaves. There were no pillows or blankets…some of the residents had no beds and slept on the floor or in wooden boxes. In some cases beds were used by one shift during the day and by others at night. There were no screens or walls to give any privacy…there were no closets or wardrobes, because each one owned only the clothing on his back.

The situation seems only to have deteriorated as the decade wore on. In his book *Smolensk under Soviet Rule* Merle Fainsod described life in Smolensk in 1937:

> The workers' barracks were described as overcrowded and in a state of extreme disrepair with water streaming from the ceiling straight onto workers' beds. Heat was rarely provided in the barracks, bedding went unchanged, and sanitary work was almost non-existent. There were no kitchens or dining halls on the construction sites; hot food could not be obtained until the evening when workers had to walk a long distance to the dining hall.

Transport too was crowded and there were shortages of water, shops and places to eat. Queues for basic commodities were long and frequent, and the government seemed to do little to ease this. In the Second Five-Year Plan there were some attempts to rectify the situation, but targets were not reached and the consumer sector was a low priority. It was difficult for central government to meet the needs of its citizens, and in the absence of a thriving small-scale entrepreneurial economy there was little chance of this changing. There was a black market in goods, and the peasants sold some of their food from their private plots in the cities, but many people had little spare cash. These were hard times. Moshe Lewin writes that conditions were ideal for the 'ruthless, the primitive, the blackmailer, the hooligan and the informer. The courts dealt with an incredible mass of cases testifying to the human destruction caused by this congestion of dwellings. The falling standards of living, the lines outside stores, and the proliferation of speculators suggest the depths of the tensions and hardships.'

Inflation put added pressure on the workers, and as prices rose, wages failed to keep up. Breakneck industrialisation created an overall climate that reduced workers' living standards. Food shortages after 1928, rising prices from 1932 and the government focus on Group A (heavy) industries as opposed to Group B (consumer) goods all hit the urban workers hard. Rationing mitigated this somewhat. The government designated 'vegetarian days' and talked of 'tightening belts' for the cause, but this was essentially window dressing for hard times and failed to impress many. In Magnitogorsk in 1932 John Scott describes the workers getting 'no meat, no butter and almost no sugar. They received only bread and a little cereal grain.' Overall conditions did not improve, and as resources switched back to defence from 1938 they declined again. The war was just round the corner and this was obviously going to cause additional widespread suffering. There was little in the way of pension or welfare provision, and if you had an accident, were ill or incapacitated you could expect little state help. Life expectancy was low and in general living conditions poor. Stalin might have stated in 1935 that 'life has become better, comrades, life has become more joyous', but he would have found it hard to get agreement from all those concerned. Overall, as Chris Ward states, 'living standards fell continuously between 1928–33, stabilised in 1934, rose throughout the "three good years" and fell back after 1936, but at no point did they recover to the late NEP levels'. He believes that the main cause of this 'was the absolute priority given by the party-state to capital investment over consumption'.

Winners and losers

Skilled workers, party members and successful managers were the 'winners' in the Five-Year Plans. They could expect decent housing, access to foreign imports, high-quality food and plenty of 'perks'. There were holiday resorts on the Black Sea that thrived in this period, and plenty of people enjoyed access to country villas (dachas), cars and a much more affluent lifestyle than they could have expected 10 years before. Foreign specialists who came to work on high-profile projects such as the Dnepr Dam also enjoyed a good quality of life (although some of them ended up joining their fellow Soviets in the dock in the show trials that started in the 1930s). Those who studied at the academies and colleges that sprang up in the 1930s to meet the demands of industrialisation also did well, and the sons and daughters of factory workers could rise up the social system by studying, working hard and joining the party.

Offsetting this, however, was the fragility of such prosperity and the fact that from 1936 onwards it was these groups that were often targeted in the purges.

The figures for those arrested, shot, exiled or imprisoned vary wildly according to different sources and the matter is the subject of intense debate. What is not disputed is that from 1936 to 1938 the purges reached a high point under Yezhov. Why Stalin decided to increase the repression of his subjects so intensely has also been debated. For whatever reason, from 1936 to 1938 the NKVD arrested and executed or imprisoned millions of Soviet citizens. Some argue that this process got out of control and that Stalin had not planned the chaos that ensued, but there can be little argument that he was aware of and supported the general idea of the purges. Although many ordinary workers and party members were sent to the camps in this period, the focus of the party leadership's attention was the middle- and high-ranking party members and also other specialist groups that could threaten or hinder Stalin. These included many engineers, technicians and managers, as well as the military and even the NKVD itself.

Yezhov, who headed the NKVD, was a party figure who had benefited from Stalin's patronage. A party secretary in Kazakhstan, he was transferred to work in the Central Committee's Department of Cadres and Assignments and then made head of the Party Control Commission. He was put in charge of the NKVD after Stalin had decided to get rid of its former chief, Yagoda (tried and executed later in 1938 for 'opposition'). Yezhov purged the NKVD of many of Yagoda's supporters and then set to work purging the army and party of supposed 'enemies of the people'. Regional and local party secretaries were arrested. Quotas were set for each district, and arrests and executions followed. In the Ukraine, for example, all 17 members of the Ukrainian government and 99 of the 102 members of the Ukrainian Central Committee were executed. These were educated people who had prospered under Communist rule, and it was such groups that suffered disproportionately in this period.

There can be little doubt that these purges affected the Five-Year Plans' efficiency. They began to seriously undermine the Third Five-Year Plan, as so many of the people who were needed to make it effective were arrested. The Council of People's Commissars (responsible for the most important government departments) lost more than 17 of its members to the purges. Their dismissal and arrest inevitably led to the arrest of all those officials lower down the chain whom they had sponsored and who were therefore charged with conspiracy. Directors of factories, chief engineers and plant managers followed in their wake, which caused untold damage to important government departments. Clearly this made economic efficiency very difficult to achieve, and the climate of fear it created can be easily imagined. Yezhov himself (like Yagoda before him) fell victim to the very process he had aided: 6 months after being replaced by his lieutenant Lavrenti Beria he was himself arrested in March 1939.

From the summer of 1939 another more pressing issue loomed. The threat from Germany became a matter of major concern. The Nazi–Soviet Pact bought Stalin a breathing space but no more. Historians have argued about how much this was an alliance of convenience for Stalin. Hitler never intended it to be anything but a temporary matter, a piece of Machiavellian realpolitik to allow him to absorb Poland into the Reich without facing a major war. Stalin, however, may have taken it more seriously. He must have realised there could never be peace with Nazi Germany, yet he behaved as if the alliance was something he could rely on. Certainly he ignored all warnings of imminent invasion in the spring of 1941, despite overwhelming evidence from spies and foreign powers that such an attack was about to be unleashed. Historian Niall Ferguson speaks of Hitler as being the one man Stalin trusted, which was unfortunate as he was a masterful liar.

As Hitler prepared his invasion, Stalin refused to allow his army to make any move that would threaten the peace. Shipments of raw materials continued to move west to Germany under the terms of the Nazi–Soviet Pact even as the panzers moved east, and there is plenty of anecdotal evidence that when Hitler attacked, Stalin had some kind of breakdown. He certainly did little for over a week, and by the time he re-emerged the USSR was facing catastrophic defeat. Stalin, though, for all his faults, was able to learn from his mistakes and gradually accepted the advice and expertise of his generals. He was lucky, as the Soviet people rallied (more out of patriotism than commitment to communism) to defend the Motherland, and he was fortunate in that the Nazis' atrocities and their treatment of the conquered territories alienated their subjects and convinced them to resist. The looming threat of war from 1939 complicates any assessment of the Third Year Plan, as rearmament took priority in its initial phase and the invasion caused it to be effectively abandoned part-way through. There can be little doubt that the first two Five-Year Plans did give the Soviet Union the industrial base from which it could resist the Germans and absorb the terrible losses in men and material that it suffered in the first year of invasion. Once the tide had turned, that industrial base also kept the Soviet army supplied with enough munitions to get it to Berlin and ensured that Hitler's dreams of European domination ended in defeat.

How much Stalin should receive credit for this achievement can be debated. It was more a victory in spite of, rather than because of, Stalin, and it was achieved at a terrible cost. Stalin was as reckless with lives in combat as he had been in collectivisation or industrialisation. Nevertheless he does deserve some credit for realising that unless the USSR modernised it would be destroyed. His path to modernity, however, was massively and needlessly costly. Collectivisation was a tremendously inefficient and terrible process that caused more problems than it solved. The achievements of the Five-Year Plans, in comparison, are more positive and in many ways are impressive. The Soviet Union by 1939 certainly had been transformed and there were many who profited in this period (although many others met with appalling and totally unjustifiable fates). The achievements of the Second and Third Five-Year Plans were overshadowed and undermined by the terrible purges of the period, with the years 1937–38 being particularly destructive. The purges undoubtedly hindered productivity and destroyed many of those whom the Soviet Union needed most: the intelligentsia. There is little justification for this terrible blood-letting; it seems to have resulted largely from Stalin's extreme paranoia and suspicion of all those around him. It is difficult to argue that Stalin's ends justified the means, but it must be acknowledged that there were some positive achievements in his rule to weigh against the many obvious negatives. What is more readily agreed is that the USSR under Stalin had been transformed from the country that he took over in 1929 and that the legacy of his rule would shape the Soviet Union's (and to some extent Europe's) history for generations to come.

Questions

1 Is it fair to say that the workers fared better than the peasants in the period 1929–41?

2 Would the Soviet Union have done better under a continuation of the NEP than it did under Stalinism?

3 Does Stalin deserve any credit for the successes of the period?

Photographs and paintings from the Stalinist era

Examining Soviet art and photography from the Stalinist era gives us a fascinating insight into the priorities of the regime and the image it wanted to project. This was a totalitarian system, in which all art and imagery was closely monitored by the authorities. Books were censored, images tightly controlled, and all aspects of the media were forced to follow the official line. The two images in this section help to highlight some of the main themes of the period. One is a painting and the other is a photograph. There is some crossover between the two media, and similar approaches can be taken to both.

The first thing you should look for is the context of the picture. This can be given by the caption, but some extra knowledge may be needed to help support your inquiry. You also need to think about the intended audience of the picture and what message it is trying to put across. What is the function of the piece? This was a system in which all official art and media were to some extent propaganda. What is propaganda? Two definitions might help. First, propaganda is the control of information, and ideas, facts or allegations spread deliberately to further a cause or to damage an opposing cause. Second, it is persuasive communication designed to influence political behaviour, usually on a large scale. In the Stalinist system all information was designed to support the regime and to undermine its enemies.

The key point to remember when looking at media sources is who produced them, and why. Understanding their function can help to open them up to analysis, and this in turn can aid your understanding of the period.

Grigory Mikhailovich Shegal's
Leader, Teacher and Friend

This painting is a famous work entitled *Leader, Teacher and Friend (Comrade Stalin at the Congress of Collective Farm Shock Workers)*, painted (oil on canvas) in 1937. It is by Grigory Mikhailovich Shegal and is an example of what became known as Socialist Realist art. It is a classic piece of Stalinist propaganda and shows how effectively the state can harness art to its own purposes.

The caption shows us immediately what type of painting this is: it is a piece of idealism. Stalin is referred to as 'Teacher, Leader and Friend' and is shown being admired and listened to by everyone at the meeting. The meeting itself is deliberately ordinary. This is no state occasion but a meeting with collective farm shock workers. Stalin here is involved with the people — he is one of them. This is something that Stalin constantly emphasised in his propaganda — he was a Soviet citizen without airs or graces or 'bourgeois pretensions'. There is also an obvious reference to him as Lenin's heir: the statue of the founder of the revolution stands above and behind him, like a statue of a religious saint. This was all part of the 'cult of Stalin' that developed in his lifetime. The importance Stalin gave to art is shown by the degree of control he exercised over it. The Socialist Realism style of painting became state policy in 1932, when Stalin issued the decree 'On the Reconstruction of Literary and Art Organisations'. The Union of Soviet Writers was founded to control the output of authors, and the new policy was rubber-stamped at the Congress of Socialist Writers in 1934. Artists who refused to toe the line or who fell out of favour could be banned from working or even shipped off to the gulag.

The aim of Socialist Realism was to support the idea that the world of work and the workers were ideal topics for art. Movements such as Impressionism and Surrealism were seen as decadent and unsuitable for painting. Art in the new socialist world would reflect the priorities of the society that produced it — it would be practical, everyday and ordinary. Its subjects would be the heroes of the new society that was emerging. They would be workers, party members and Bolshevik leaders. Above all, Stalin would be the central figure: Stalin as hero, leader, wise teacher, the subject of adoration and respect, the true heir of Lenin and protector of the Bolshevik legacy. As the Statute of the Union of Soviet Writers in 1934 stated:

> Socialist realism is the basic method of Soviet literature and literary criticism. It demands of the artist the truthful, historically concrete representation of reality in its revolutionary development. Moreover, the truthfulness and historical concreteness of the artistic representation of reality must be linked with the task of ideological transformation and education of workers in the spirit of socialism.

Art, like everything else in the USSR, was part of the state and under strict control — it was not about pleasure but about supporting the aims of the revolution.

'Bolsheviks instructing peasants in the benefits of collectivisation'

This photograph is typical of many published around the time of the collectivisation campaign, aimed at demonstrating the popularity of the scheme and encouraging peasants to join in. This type of photo is easier to approach and to understand than the painting, as there is no subtle agenda. This is pure propaganda — a staged event where peasants are being told the benefits of collectivisation and appear to be listening attentively and with enthusiasm. We know little about the context of this photo, other than that it was taken during the collectivisation campaign. It is clear, though, that it is designed to show the process of collectivisation as civilised, carefully planned and generally supported. The reality of mass arrests, deportations and famines is not shown. Instead the Bolshevik activists giving the presentation are surrounded by photos and paintings of leading Bolsheviks and are portrayed as reasonable and civilised. A common mistake that students make when approaching photographic material is to assume that it is somehow more 'reliable' than a painting or memoir. Photos can be changed, manipulated or partial, and so should be treated with the same analytical skills (and a certain degree of scepticism) as any other sources. This is particularly the case in Stalin's Soviet Union at the height of collectivisation and the Five-Year Plans, when the whole state was engaged in pushing the country into the modern era by any means necessary.

Five-Year Plans: an overview

First Five-Year Plan (October 1928–December 1932)

Focus

Heavy industries: coal, iron, oil, steel, electricity, cement, metals and timber. Some 1,500 new enterprises were opened and these sectors absorbed 80% of state investment.

Successes

Electricity production trebled.
Coal and iron output doubled.
Steel production increased by a third.
Engineering industry developed.
New industrial complexes built or started and new tractor factories multiplied to deal with demands of collectivisation.

Weaknesses

Little investment in consumer goods.
Small workshops went bust.
Chemicals targets were not met.
Skilled workers were in short supply.

Overall

The Soviet economy enjoyed impressive growth.

Second Five-Year Plan (January 1933–December 1937)

Focus

The emphasis shifted to communications and investment in rail links was massive. Some 4,500 new enterprises were started.

Successes

Some big projects such as Dneprostroy Dam in use.
Electricity production increased rapidly.
Machine-making and metalworking improved.
Chemical industries grew.
Metallurgy developed — zinc, copper and tin were mined.

Weaknesses

Consumer goods still received little investment.
Oil production still weak.

Overall

This was a period in which initial progress was consolidated. The years 1934–36 were probably the best, with production increasing and the large-scale purges yet to start.

Third Five-Year Plan (January 1938–June 1941)

Focus

Rearmament and heavy industry.

Successes

Defence sector grew.
Heavy industry continued to expand.

Weaknesses

Steel and oil production still lagged behind targets.
Consumers were still low priority.
Purges began to affect productivity, with skilled managers and workers being sent to the gulag or executed.

Overall

A bad winter in 1938 affected food production and the threat of war distorted targets. Gosplan was badly affected by purges, and Stalin's elimination of the army high command further complicated matters. The Plan was halted by the Nazi invasion in June 1941.

Timeline

1922 Stalin appointed General Secretary of the Bolshevik Party

1924 Lenin dies; power struggle begins

1927 Trotsky, Zinoviev and Kamenev expelled from the party. In December at Fifteenth Party Congress Stalin announces First Five-Year Plan

1928 War fear as relations with Poland and France deteriorate after diplomatic relations with Britain are broken off

1929 Stalin is undisputed leader of the party. He has won the power struggle

1930 Stalin announces 25% of the grain producing areas in the USSR will be collectivised by the end of the year

1932 In December the First Five-Year Plan is ended a year ahead of schedule with official pronouncements of success

1933 Second Five-Year Plan announced

1934 Seventy per cent of peasant households collectivised. Famine in the Ukraine and other parts of the USSR has caused up to 7 million deaths
Purges begin; initially they focus on party but spread to all areas of life.

1935 Alexei Stakhanov cuts 102 tons of coal in one shift (almost 16 times the norm)

1936 New Constitution adopted: guarantees full civil liberties. Ninety per cent of peasant households collectivised

1938 Third Five-Year Plan starts. Purges reach their peak

1939 Nazi–Soviet Pact precedes invasion of Poland.

1940 Soviet Union invades Baltic states and Finland

1941 Nazi Germany invades Soviet Union. Third Five-Year Plan abandoned

1943 Surrender of German Sixth Army at Stalingrad; war turns in Stalin's favour

1945 Germany surrenders. Soviet Union one of two world superpowers

1949 Soviet Union explodes atom bomb

1953 Stalin dies

Further reading

Alan Bullock, *Hitler and Stalin* (Fontana Press 1991)

This book's comparative approach may annoy some scholars but it remains a classic work on both Stalin and Hitler. The fact that more recent scholars such as Richard Overy and Michael Burleigh continue to explore elements of similarity and difference between the two regimes demonstrates that there is still mileage in such comparisons. Bullock remains hard to beat for students wanting a readable, lucid account of totalitarian Europe. This comparative approach allows fruitful conclusions to be drawn. Bullock writes on p. 1077:

> Defeat [in the Second World War] cost the German people a terrible price, but at least it spared them — and the world — the perpetuation of the Nazi regime. Victory cost the Russians an even greater price but did not liberate them…Instead of relaxing he [Stalin] renewed his demands upon the Russian people; the old suspicion and distrust returned…The Stalinist system which he had fastened on the Russian people continued to shackle their energies and deny them freedom for more than another thirty-five years.

Orlando Figes, *A People's Tragedy: the Russian Revolution 1891–1924* (Pimlico 1996)

While this book deals with the early years of Bolshevik rule (in fact it finishes with the death of Lenin in 1924), it is nevertheless crucial to any understanding of Stalin and his regime. Whether Stalinism was a refinement or bastardisation of Leninism is still very much under discussion, but it is undeniable that the foundation of the Bolshevik regime created many of the problems that Stalin tried to resolve, and an appreciation of that context is essential. Figes is an excellent writer and this book is one of the most readable accounts of the period in print. He is unsparing in his criticism of the Bolshevik experiment, and after reading his book you can understand why! A sample of his conclusion on p. 823 shows this:

> The Russian Revolution launched a vast experiment in social engineering — perhaps the grandest in the history of mankind. It was arguably an experiment the human race was bound to make at some point in its evolution, the logical conclusion of humanity's historic striving for social justice and comradeship…The experiment went horribly wrong, not so much because of the malice of its leaders, most of whom had started out with the highest ideals, but because their ideals were themselves impossible.

Chris Ward, *Stalin's Russia* (Hodder Arnold 2005)

This is an excellent overview of the latest historiographical and scholarly thinking on Stalin and his regime. There is plenty of statistical support for Ward's assertions, and he has the advantage of the latest Russian archival research that has emerged since the end of the Soviet regime in 1991. There are also plenty of sections on interpretations and evaluations of Stalin, and Ward is not afraid to challenge conventional thinking on Stalin and his place in history. This is evident in his concluding chapter. He writes on pp. 264–65:

> We need to remind ourselves of the purpose of academic history. It is not to establish a mythic truth. Nor is it to point a moral tale. Nor is it to praise winners and condemn losers, or vice versa. Hard enough and imperfect though the attempt must always be, historians should try to see all round a problem; to understand and make comprehensible old policies, old factions and past lives.

He expands this point on p. 267:

> By and large to this day the academic community — in the West and in the lands of the old regime — still fails one of the primary tests of the historian's craft: to disengage from partisan strife and to see Stalin, Stalinism and Stalinist society as products of their time.

Terry Fiehn and Chris Corin, *Communist Russia under Lenin and Stalin* (SHP Advanced History Core Texts, Hodder Murray 2002)

This user-friendly, up-to-date textbook is aimed at A-level students making the transition from GCSE and is an excellent overview of the period. Historical debates are succinctly summarised, and it includes plenty of snappy quotes, pithy comment, and material from recently opened archives to help students make up their own mind about what happened. There are also plenty of pictures, diagrams and activities to break up the text. The authors' examination of whether Stalin's rule can be compared with that of the tsars is typically concise. On p. 136 they write:

> There is a strong case for arguing that the traditions of Russian history preceding the revolution played an important role in determining the shape and character of Stalinism. The Stalinist state that emerged in the 1930s had many similarities with the tsarist state of the nineteenth century…That is not to say that Stalinism was somehow inevitable. What is suggested is that, given the chaotic and difficult circumstances in which the Russians found themselves, they retreated or slipped into traditional solutions which they understood well and with which they were familiar.

Simon Sebag Montefiore, *Stalin: The Court of the Red Tsar* (Phoenix 2004)

While not an academic in the conventional sense, Simon Sebag Montefiore has achieved no mean feat with this book on Stalin and his inner circle: he shows us a Stalin with charm! This is a Stalin very different from the tyrant in the Kremlin that most of us imagine; instead a much more human figure emerges. This was a Stalin who shared open house with various other Old Bolsheviks in the Kremlin in the early 1930s and who achieved power because he was popular as well as crafty. It is a shock to be presented with this sometimes genial Stalin, and this is a book that takes us into the personal web of relationships around the leader of Bolshevik Russia in the late 1920s and early 1930s. An extract from the book on p. 39 demonstrates this well:

> Stalin often dropped in on his neighbours the Kaganoviches for a chess game. Natasha Andreyeva remembers Stalin frequently putting his head round the door looking for her parents: 'Is Andrei here or Dora Moisevna?' Sometimes he wanted to go to the cinema but her parents were late, so she went with Stalin herself. When Mikoyan needed something, he would simply cross the courtyard and knock on Stalin's door, where he would be invited in for dinner…When Stalin was on holiday, this merry band continually dropped in on Nadya (his wife) to send her husband messages and political gossip.

Martin Amis, *Koba the Dread* (Jonathan Cape 2002) and Simon Sebag Montefiore, *My Affair with Stalin* (Phoenix 1997)

These two books are included together as they are suitable for those students who do not feel like wading into an academic text or for those who have been wading through such texts and want some light relief. Martin Amis's book, an excellent examination of Stalinism and its relationship with British left-wing writers and academics, is easy to read and covers lots of interesting ideas. Sebag Montefiore's work is a comic interpretation of Stalin through the eyes and actions of an 11-year-old at prep school and is both clever and amusing (a rare combination in historical writing). It's surreal, but then by all accounts so was life in Stalinist Russia. An extract from p. 129 might give some flavour of the book:

> After Pelham, the purge was no longer fun. It was real. And it had a life of its own. The denunciations and tortures came quicker and quicker. When did it begin to spin out of control? When did the Politburo begin to merge with the life of the school so that the edges became fatally blurred? Every day after prep, Petty recounted the atrocities committed in my name….

Glossary

Bolsheviks

The faction of the Russian Social Democratic Labour Party that split from its parent party in 1903 and dedicated itself to the overthrow of the tsarist system. Became the Russian Communist Party in 1918.

Cheka

Russian acronym for 'Extraordinary Commission' (full name: Extraordinary Commission for Combating Counter-Revolution and Sabotage). It was responsible for destroying all opposition to the Bolsheviks.

Comintern

Short for '**Com**munist **Intern**ational', an organisation set up in March 1919 to spread communism to other European countries and to support Communist parties abroad. Sometimes known as the Third International.

commissar

The Bolshevik term for what we would understand as a government minister. Often responsible for a department or area of policy.

Gosplan

The state planning agency, responsible for setting targets and quotas and generally overseeing the Five-Year Plans.

gulag

Russian acronym for the Main Administration of Corrective Labour Camps, a branch of the state security agency. This was the organisation responsible for running the vast network of labour camps maintained by the Bolsheviks.

ideologue

A person who acts according to the demands of a theory or ideology regardless of whether it is a practical or justifiable action. To some extent collectivisation was a process driven by ideological considerations as well as economic ones. It was a Marxist solution to the problems posed by the peasants to the party leadership.

kolkhoz

The main type of collective farm (there was also the *toz* and the *sovkhoz*). Its members owned it collectively. An elected council ran it and land was farmed as one unit, with a quota payable to the state every year. Peasant households were allowed to keep a small private plot of land.

kulak

Traditionally a label applied to wealthier peasants. Became a catch-all term to describe anyone that the Bolshevik regime deemed to be an enemy during the collectivisation process.

mir

The term used to describe the peasant communities in pre-revolutionary Russia. The word also meant 'world', 'peace' and 'universe' in peasant Russian. The *'mir'* was governed by an assembly of peasant elders who controlled all aspects of village life.

MTS

Machine and Tractor Station. A state-owned depot where agricultural machinery such as tractors and combine harvesters could be leased to collective farms. Often had the Bolshevik regional party leadership and/or NKVD units attached.

NKVD

People's Commissariat for Internal Affairs. Successor to the *Cheka* and OGPU. It emerged in 1934 to succeed previous internal security agencies. It was succeeded by the Ministry of State Security (MGB) in 1946.

OGPU

Successor to the GPU, which succeeded the *Cheka*. Another mutation of the secret police the Bolsheviks were so fond of employing.

Orgburo

The organisational body that ran the Communist Party when the Central Executive Committee was not meeting. It was linked to the Politburo and the Secretariat.

plenum

An assembly. The term usually refers to the Plenum of the Central Committee of the Communist Party, which was a small group of leading party officials.

Politburo

The Political Bureau of the Central Committee of the VKP (the All-Union Communist Party). This was the nerve centre of the Bolshevik regime and typically had eight to ten members.

pragmatist

A person who acts according to the demands of the situation rather than according to any theory. The adoption of the NEP was a pragmatic solution to the problems Lenin faced in 1921.

soviet

The term used to describe councils elected by groups of workers, soldiers and/or peasants. They first appeared in the 1905 revolution and then again in 1917. Larger councils often ran the cities after the February Revolution. The Provisional Government was forced to share power with the Petrograd Soviet. The Bolshevik takeover of the soviets was crucial to their success in the October Revolution.

Sovnarkom

Council of People's Commissars. This was the executive branch of government in the Soviet Union and equivalent to a modern cabinet, but it effectively had to do what the Politburo decided.

syndicates

These were associations of businesses grouped together during the Five-Year Plans for organisational purposes. This enabled the government to set targets and supervise them more easily.

totalitarian

A system of government that regulates all aspects of life for those living in it. The government has 'total' control over its subjects.

USSR

Union of Soviet Socialist Republics, formally established in 1922. More commonly known as the Soviet Union. Russia was merely one — though much the largest — of ultimately 15 republics in the USSR.

VKP

All-Union Communist Party: the official name of the Bolshevik Party after 1925.

zek

A slang term in Russian for prisoner or 'inmate' — usually taken to refer to those sent to the gulags in Stalin's time but originally an acronym for those working on the Belomor Canal between 1931 and 1933.

YALE COLLEGE
LEARNING RESOURCE CENTRE